Death *of* State

WILL SUTTER

Palmetto Publishing Group
Charleston, SC

Death of State
Copyright © 2019 by Will Sutter

First Edition

Printed in the United States

ISBN-13: 978-1-64111-435-6
ISBN-10: 1-64111-435-5

CHAPTER ONE

AN INCONVENIENT BODY

John Stapelton was on his back staring up at Alexander Hamilton. "Somebody making a statement" Detective Barody asked. He looked around to see if anyone laughed.

The statue of Hamilton, first treasurer of the United States, stood like an exclamation point at the foot of the Treasury steps. It was an odd place for a body. But this was DC, 51st state and capital city of the United States. Citizens took politics in with their morning Wheaties.

Detective Barody was actually a little ahead of himself. There were no marks on the body to indicate foul play. It was only after the autopsy that John Stapleton became the subject of a murder investigation. The Novichok on his lips, the good detective concluded, hadn't got there because he was using the wrong shaving lotion.

The Defense Department had exclusive control of the deadly substance. "Makes it a federal case," Detective Barody said, closing his notebook.

Mike Sullivan leaned back to get a better look at the Potomac thundering over Great Falls. He had the blanket as close as possible to the Falls without getting wet, so close he had to tilt his head slightly up. Louise watched him closely.

It was a couple of months now they had been socializing. Before that they were just colleagues, too busy for much of a social life. She was the Prime Minister's daughter and he was his special assistant. Slowly, they found they enjoyed one another's company; proximity at work made the rest easy. And now, on this trip out to Great Falls, she felt something more than just liking, something deeper stirring, something not there before.

On this balmy Saturday September afternoon she was finding it not just pleasantly convenient to be close to him but exciting. As they walked down the C&O tow path from Fisherman's Inn to the falls, their shoulders touched whenever they hit a rough patch on the path's gritty, hard surface. He made no effort to move away. She knew she'd accept an invitation back to his place for a drink if offered.

She leaned back with him on the blanket and felt the exciting warmth of his body touching hers. Since her divorce several years back, there were few occasions to enjoy real male warmth. Emotional scars and work had seen to that. Mike was a happy discovery.

His cell phone rang.

"Shit," he muttered, as disturbed as she was just when things were going nicely. A playful kiss was just over the horizon.

"I have to answer," he apologized. It was his on-call phone with Blair House. He had turned off his personal phone to preserve whatever magic these moments might create.

"Mike," the voice said evenly. "Hope I'm not interrupting anything important."

There was only one answer to such a question from the Prime Minister of the United States.

"A small matter has just come up. It needs to be addressed."

"A "small" matter to Jim Stevens was a full blown crises to just about anyone else.

"I'll" be there as soon as I can. I'm at Great Falls. Be about half an hour."

"Fine," the voice said. "Come directly here."

"Sorry," he said to Louise. "That was your Dad. Something's up."

"Isn't it always?" she asked a little desperately. She knew better than to ask. Whatever "was up" was not something to be discussed in unclassified settings.

The block of Pennsylvania Ave. between 16th and 17TH Streets was home to both the White House and just across the street Blair House the official residence and office of the Prime Minister. Offices for his staff, much smaller than White House staffs had been, were in adjacent town houses fronting on Lafayette Park. Blair House was the Downing Street of the US.

The block was kept traffic free by potted tree barriers at either end, pedestrians only. Vehicles, bombs on wheels to the secret service, were routed around by H Street or Constitution Ave, too far for any blast to reach the White House.

The president still occupied the Executive Mansion, but the office was now ceremonial as in most parliamentary democracies. The executive power of the government rested in a cabinet of ministers led by the prime minister, all drawn from the House of Representatives.

The change to a parliamentary system was precipitated by the disastrous administration of the Great Pretender, as the real estate magnate from Manhattan had been called.

Realizing it was no longer well served by the political devises of the 18th century, the "People" changed how it elected and got rid of its leaders. Impeachment was too cumbersome and legalistic. Political need be had to be given its place to keep the rare mountebank who might capture the office from doing fatal damage.

Mike entered through the Lafayette Park entrance of one of the two brick row houses on Lafayette Park that housed the offices of the Prime Minister's staff. Blair House itself, the 19th century yellow brick residence on Pennsylvania Avenue, had been the home of Lincoln's post master general, Montgomery Blair, hence the name. Most recently it had been the official guest house of the government. The two row houses held working spaces for the prime minister's office. The cabinet room where the prime minister met almost weekly with his cabinet was on the second floor of Blair House.

The Prime Minister' office in Blair House was in a pleasant, sunny corner room overlooking both leafy Lafayette Park with General Andrew Jackson on his war horse, and the White House opposite. Jackson stared straight into the Prime Minister's corner window.

"Spying?" Jim muttered upon first seeing the office.

"Can't be," Mike replied. "Jackson was near sighted."

Jim laughed.

Nothing like a smile on the PM's face now as Mike politely knocked on his office door and entered. It was a Saturday. The Prime minister was casually dressed in a polo shirt and shorts.

"Thought I'd take a walk along the canal tow path later in the afternoon. Then this came up," he said pointing to the phone he had just used to call Mike.

The 19ᵗʰ C&O Canal linked Georgetown with Cumberland, Maryland, over a hundred miles away. The part of its tree rimmed tow path in Georgetown was a favorite with hikers and joggers, green starved city dwellers refreshed by glimpses of the Potomac and the Virginia palisades across the river. Its popularity made it an impossible security nightmare for presidential security details.

The office of prime minister was not so encumbered. James Duncan Stevens suited up in shorts and a polo shirt for a stroll along the tow path on a sunny weekend afternoon was in no way remarkable. He was just one more citizen, though an easily recognized one. People gave him space. Only two security guards were needed. He carried none of the Augustan trappings of THE PRESIDENT OF THE UNITED STATES.

The telephone was the only object on the PM's otherwise clean desk. For a man who was unorthodox and not made uncomfortable by new thinking, Jim Stevens kept a clean, tidy desk. It was a subject of running humor between himself and his special assistant.

"What do you do with all that paper that streams into this office?" Mike would ask.

"In the waste basket," the Prime Minister would reply with a wicked glint. "If it's important, they'll send it again. If not, why bother?"

It was an empty joke. Most of the paperwork never reached Blair House. Work that once had been concentrated in the White House was now spread throughout the various departments of government, a more collegial and efficient arrangement. The executive branch was no longer a separate branch of government but an extension of the House of which most ministers were members. The cabinet operated as a college under the general supervision of the prime minister who set the policy and had the final word. When he didn't, he resigned.

"Just got a call from the Metropolitan Police. Seems a certain John Stapleton turned up dead at the foot of Alexander Hamilton's statue in front of Treasury."

"Really?" Mike asked, puzzled. Most deaths in the capital city did not involve the prime minister's office. Even if it were a federal matter, the FBI would have the action.

"Novichok was found on the body."

That clarified things. Novichok was Russian. It hadn't been used since the kleptocratic KGB regime of Vladimir Putin. But he was no longer in office. A fatal cerebral aneurism had seen to that, deeply ironic for a man who made such a pubic fetish of radiant health.

His replacement, Vitali Kataev, was a reformer in the mold of Gorbachev. Russia's future, in his vison, lay in cooperation rather than antagonism with the West, Russia a member in good standing of the 21st century world. Either that or reduction to the moldering status of those failing Arab regimes whose glories were sighted only in backward glances, fruits of the autocratic past. He had healthier ambitions for Russia.

Prime Minister Jim Sevens was taking active steps to cooperate. "Why at this hopeful time would the Russians do such a destructive thing?"

The question did not need to be asked aloud.

"Something is not right," the Prime Minister muttered. "Vasyli Kataev is not stupid and he's not two faced. So why this?"

The question, Mike knew, was rhetorical. He hadn't been summoned to answer it, or even help. Not at this point.

"Soo, you want me to . . . ?"

"Go over to the police precinct that handles federal issues. Find out what you can. I plan to call a cabinet meeting Monday to discuss the matter. It would be disastrous if our negotiations with Kataev were derailed by this."

CHAPTER TWO

IT'S THE RUSSIANS, WHO ELSE?

Detective Ralph Barody was just over medium height, thin and dressed in clothes that barely escaped shabby. He had a lean, tight face with a perpetual expression of deep disappointment with a world that stubbornly refused to amend its errant way. So it had to deal with Detective Barody. He regarded himself as a defender of righteousness, though he would never say that out loud. "Putting assholes away," was how he described it.

His office was in the special precinct building on 23rd Street near the State Department and convenient to the White House and its neighbor, Blair House.

"How can I help you?" he said to Mike as he was ushered into Barody's second floor office overlooking 23rd Street and the narrow, leafy island that split the street in two, giving it an air of European elegance. The row houses lining the broad street had the same elevated tone, a boulevard with pretensions above those of its more pedestrian neighbors. The row houses were designed with senior members of the government bureaucracy in mind. That day had passed and many of the row houses now were now broken up into apartments though trendy, pricey ones preserving the street's privileged air.

"The body found in front of Treasury," Mike said without preamble. He assumed this sharp faced detective knew who he was. He also looked like the kind of man who liked to get right down to cases. "I'm told traces of Novichok were found."

"You're told right," Detective Barody said. "On his lips. Fortunately for the officers examining his body, yours truly included, we wore latex gloves. None of it got on any of us. Fucking Russians," he concluded.

"You're sure it's Russian?"

Detective Barody shrugged. "Who else? Only the Russians use that shit. FSB, Russian mafia . . . ? Who knows?"

"And the cause of death was Novichok?"

Had Mike not been from the prime minister's office, Detective Barody might have loosed a dart from his rich reservoir of sarcasm, reserved for "government assholes." On his mind was 'with Novichok what the fuck more do you need?' What came out was "That's our working hypothesis. We don't have an autopsy report yet. But with traces of Novichok present on his lips . . . ?" He gave a detective shrug.

Mike saw the point. "Anything else you can tell me. I'm sure you understand the political implications of this?"

He did, the good detective being a member of the Metropolitan Police's federal unit, an elite squad that handled cases with serious political implications. Any congressman found dead in the bed of some woman not his lawfully wedded wife often required a certain delicatesse in the handling. He's retired from the State Department. A cookie pusher. I expect this might complicate our relations with the Russkies. Too bad, you ask me. Don't understand why your boss thinks he can trust them. But that's for you to worry about, not me. I'm just a cop." He gave Mike a big smile that seemed to say fuck you.

CHAPTER THREE

WHAT TOOK SO LONG?

"I'm glad you asked me back," she said, resting her head on the pillow propped against the headboard, her eyes dreamy from what she had to admit was about the best love for some time. She felt cared for more than ravished. Who knew Mike could be so tender?

"Wasn't sure you'd say yes," he replied half apologetically.

She let that lay there. Not say yes? Hardly. But instinct told her a little doubt was always a good thing. She gave him an enigmatic smile.

He didn't care. It *had* been good love, their first. He was still amazed how closely they seemed to have melded. Before, she always seemed distant, friendly, but distant, a shining other perched on an unclimbable mountain. Suddenly they were in bed, the mountain unaccountably surmounted. He was too happy to think about the wonder of it all.

They had been to a Nats' game. Someone was always leaving Nats' game tickets at the prime minister's office. Most were usually donated to some worthy children's cause around town. But staff were occasionally allowed to take advantage. Mike worried if it was right to do so. The hint of bribery seemed to hover like the odor of bad cheese. Mike had a keen sense of the difference between acceptable and none. But such goodies weren't given back, if not used. Mike didn't know who left them, and so far as he could see, no strings were attached. Jim Stevens, for one, would never abide that. Besides, Mike needed a way to make up for their arrested sojourn at Great Falls. It was time he and Louise became more than what they had been.

The seats were right behind the Nats' dugout, just about as good as there were, saving seats reserved for major league scouts behind home plate, better if you were scouting a pitcher and wanted to see his stuff.

He thought he might have to explain a lot of things to Louise.

But it turned out she knew as much as he did about baseball. Back in their native Lexington, Kentucky, where Jim Stevens had been the popular mayor, Louise regularly attended Wild Cats baseball games at the University of Kentucky and those of the Legends, the Double AA team of the major league Astros. Louise knew her baseball. That made the whole evening easier.

It was made easier still by a Nats' victory, convincingly and satisfyingly secured in the last of the ninth by a three run explosion in a 5 to 2 game. As they headed for his apartment four blocks away with a bounce in their step he jauntily asked, "come back for a drink?"

"Thought you'd never ask," she replied.

They made small talk about the game as they walked. As soon as his apartment door was closed, he knew what to do. Actually, they started on the elevator. Inside, he slipped off the sweater she was wearing against the cool night air, put his arms around her waist and kissed her lightly on the neck. She twisted around and kissed him fiercely on the mouth. After that it was a blur until they were totally without clothing and face to face in his queen size bed. The rest needn't be talked about.

The first time Mike took notice of Louise as a woman and not just Jim's daughter she was walking in front of him on Pennsylvania Avenue toward Blair House.

Mike didn't realize it was Louise. He was admiring the lilt in this woman's walk, a liveliness that made him want to look more. As soon she mounted the front steps to Blair House, he noted the fashionable boots hugging her shapely ankles, light brown leather as fine as silk, a perfect complement to the full skirt dropping just below her knees. The sight made Mike suck in his breath, wondering who she was. Then he realized who it was. He had never seen Louise so stylishly dressed before. Usually she was dressed soberly in what Mike privately called her lawyer's weeds. The boots and flared skirt were far from lawyer's weeds.

"Not bad" for a forty old woman, he thought.

From that day on his feelings for her were an unsettled mix of eroticism, friendship and collegiality.

CHAPTER FOUR

THE COMBAT BEGINS

Congressman Spurlock had the floor.

"Mr. Speaker, I call attention to this morning's police report that says a body was found last night in front of the US Treasury on Pennsylvania Avenue. According to the report, Mr. Speaker, the body contained traces of the deadly nerve agent Novichok. I ask this house, Mr. Speaker, if it knows which nation among the circle of so called civilized nations, Mr. Speaker, has ever used this particular nerve agent as a weapon against human beings. It is Russia, Mr. Speaker, Russia, the very same nation that developed this deadly agent, the very same nation, the only nation, that has ever used it against its enemies. I remind this house, Mr. Speaker, of the case of the defected Russian spy Skripal who was residing in Great Britain with his daughter. Both of them almost died after attacked with Novichok. Mr. Speaker, the United States does not possess Novichok, nor, to the best of my knowledge does any other nation. Only the Russian Federated Republic possesses it and only it has used this despicable device against human beings. "

"Does the honorable gentleman from Kentucky have a point he wishes to make with this report? Otherwise why not just place it in the record so we can move on? I remind the honorable gentleman from Kentucky that the house has many important measures before it that beg its attention, the most pressing, proposed changes to the National Health Care and Retirement Act."

"I indeed do have a point, Mr. Speaker. As this house well knows, the government of James D Stevens is at this very moment engaged in negotiations to improve relations with our age old enemy, Russia, and . . . "

"The chair is well aware of that, Mr. Spurlock. Is there a proposal to this house hidden in all your superheated verbiage?"

"There is indeed, Mr. Speaker. I propose that this house task the committee of foreign relations to open an immediate investigation into the matter as it may affect the legitimacy and soundness of the government's efforts to befriend a nation that has never wished us well. I propose the question."

"The question will not be proposed at this time, Mr. Spurlock. The chair believes it advisable to wait until more facts are developed and the government has had a chance to comment. I point out there is nothing to keep you from raising this question with the Prime Minister and members of his cabinet at the question period next week".

Congressman Spurlock did not expect his motion to carry. It was simply the first shot in a new iteration of his unending war with Prime Minister, James Duncan Stevens.

Any journalist in town could have described to any interested visitor from abroad the nature of the relationship between Congressman Gilbert Spurlock and Prime Minister Stevens. It went back to their days in Kentucky when Jim Stevens was Governor of Kentucky and Gil Spurlock was an assemblyman from western Kentucky, a man of obvious southern roots. To Gil Spurlock's conservative eyes, Jim Stevens was a rank Socialist out to subvert the country's independent soul and make it a nation of welfare bums.

Both men were elected to the national congress, where Spurlock continued his attacks. Stevens became leader of the Americrats, progressives who had split from the old Democratic Party. He led the fight to rationalize the nation's health care and retirement systems. Medicare had been extended to all who had no other insurance though a government option. But coverage was still not universal. The inadequacies of

Social Security brought on a national crises when a large number of retired seniors suffered severe reductions to their monthly checks though various forms of chicanery by the companies funding their pensions.

Jim fought the election, grasping the twin horns of the crises by proposing a national plan giving every citizen cradle to grave health care coverage and a secure and decent retirement. The combined programs were to be paid for by a national VAT.

He won big, and as leader of the party with the most votes in congress, he worked out a coalition with the old Democrats to become prime minister of a coalition government.

Prime Minister Stevens asked Mike to talk to the Russian embassy, but quietly and discretely. "Spurlock already has a spotlight on this. No need for more attention. The Russians may well deny it. It's important how they deny it"

Mike could have picked up the phone and gotten right through to the Russian ambassador, Pavel Alexandrovich Novisty. But that could get out in a town whose nose for gossip was as keen as a hound's. That the special assistant to Prime Minister Stevens had called on the Russian ambassador would be a juicy little news tidbit, especially right after the body of a retired American diplomat with service in Moscow is found dead, traces of Novichok present. It wasn't yet general news, but enough of it was already out to feed a handful of insiders. The word would soon be wide spread. A call by Mike on Ambassador Novisty and a body showing traces of Novichok would quickly be mixed into an interesting little speculative stew, a dietary staple in a town of chatterers and pundits.

A call from the special assistant's office to the Russian embassy on Friendship Heights using a secure line that even the FBI did not tap quickly set up a meeting, casual, informal and discrete. Elam Ivanovich Klimov was not part of the embassy's intelligence apparat. State, the FBI and the CIA all said he was not FSB. But he was a man who had most of the threads of the embassy in his hands. It was known that Pavel Alexandrovich Novisty-wire taps can at times be wonderful things-relied heavily on Klimov's advice.

The meeting took place at a little country tavern in Warrenton, Virginia, well away from prying eyes. Both men used rented cars that bore no plates or other marks suggesting high level government or diplomatic officials.

Klimov, tall rather than not, had the long, lean, sharp featured face and the long, straight, sandy hair of a Russian intellectual who smoked too many cigarettes and had little regard for a healthy diet. Mike found him seated in an out of the way alcove. Both were dressed in chinos and polo shirts, golfing buddies meeting for lunch after the last round. The golf course was called "The Madison" after James Madison, constitutional architect and fourth US president. His estate, Montpelier, was nearby

Mike already knew Klimov. As a convenient way into the office of the Prime Minister for anyone looking for an informal, unstructured conversation, Mike was an oft used channel for those sudden little freshets of information springing up in a city that governed a large nation and was first among the equals of world democracies.

After a meeting at an embassy reception to show off a new Russia film, Mike knew Elam well enough to ask a personal question.

"Elam. It's an unusual name. Is it Russian?"

Klimov laughed. "It is a most Russian name from a certain era, though not as common as Ivan or Mikhail or Vladimir. It is an acronym-ELAM for Leninism, Electrification and Hydroelectric power. I was born in the time of Communism and my parents, like so many other parents of that time, chose names that expressed certain communist ideals. So I am Elam, Mr. Leninism and Electrification. But my friends call me Elam, and I wish you would."

"So, Elam," Mike now said, "you always seem to be first. Do you live near Warrenton?"

Elam grinned. "Since you are from the prime minister's office, I must always be the first, no? Good protocol."

"I'll buy that," Mike said. He liked Elam, felt relaxed with him. Russians, he had discovered, liked it when people got personal with them in an informal, friendly way. It didn't mean they always gave you what you wanted, but they said no nicely.

"So we are speaking about Mr. Stapleton, unless I miss my guess," Elam said.

"Right, as usual," Mike replied. They wouldn't need to go all the way to Warrenton to discuss the usual matters under discussion between the Embassy of the Russia Republic and the US. "The PM is puzzled. He is hoping Russia is not involved. The reasons are obvious."

"And I can confidently say no for reasons that we hope are equally obvious. You are thinking the Novichok means Russia?"

"It's been mentioned," Mike replied.

"But the US has stocks of Novichok. Am I not correct?"

"If we do, you know something I don't," Mike said.

"No matter. I can say in total sincerity, the government of Russia is not involved. President Kataev is committed to the course laid out by him and Prime Minister Steven. It is in the best interests of both countries. We have totally abandoned the Putin line. We want good relations with you. That is not something President Kataev will jeopardize. I am authorized to assure you it is not us."

"No rogue elements of the FSB?" Mike asked. It was a serious question.

"There are reports not all elements of the FSB are totally on board with President Kataev's opening to the West.

The FSB referred to is the successor to the KGB, the Russian initials standing for Federalniya Slusbe Besapastnisty-the Federal Security Service.

"Such reports are correct," Elam said. His reply was a refreshing sign of the changes happening in the New Russia, as President Kataev called it. At one time no Russian official would have made such an admission, true or not, so deeply was the habit of secrecy with foreigners ingrained in the Russian character.

"Can you be certain some rogue is not involved? Prime Minister Stevens' government is as serious as President Kataev about improving relations with Russia, and he is ready to work around any rogue involvement. I know you are aware Representative Spurlock has already raised the issue on the House floor to embarrass the government. More will follow unless we can show convincingly that Russia's hands are clean."

"Hundred percent assurance, no. Only ninety five percent assurance that no FSB or other kind of Russian rogue is involved. Russia is going through many positive changes, but we haven't yet lost the habit of keeping close check on bad elements, inside or outside Russia. I can assure you no Russia of the government is involved in Mr. Stapleton's demise. If a rogue is discovered, we will deal with him expeditiously and make public statements to that effect. There has been no change in our policy."

Mike didn't ask Elam if the Russian organs-how they referred to their security services-still employed mokry deyla, wet stuff, the usual way of dealing with traitors. Wet meant blood. Relations weren't that good yet.

Mike's report was reassuring.

I trust Vitali enough at this point to think he wouldn't permit such a thing," Jim Stevens said. "But until we find out who killed Stapleton with Novichok, we won't be able to shut Spurlock up. He can't force us to hold hearings, but he can keep bringing the matter on the floor. I'm sure it will be central in the question period next week. In the meantime, let's keep on the police to find the killer."

MIKE AND LOUISE GET COMFORTABLE

Louise wondered if she might have taken the initiative if Mike hadn't. To keep on dating the way they were, movies-dinner, trips to Great Falls and other local spots of interest-seemed pointless. She wanted more and she was sure Mike did as well. She noticed the way he looked at her every so often. She knew, also, that she was dressing differently because of him. What he had called her lawyer's weeds - a confession he made after they were intimate - were a thing of the past. It was how she dressed when she was still a partner at Schnabel, Ebley and Martin, Lexington's leading law firm, at least by their lights. Her wardrobe gradually changed after Mike entered her life, a little less law lady and a little more come hither, nothing showy or obvious, but noticeable to those who could see. She was happy he had.

She was still too young-forty one-to condemn herself to a life time of celibacy, and marriage, for a whole host of reasons, did not seem a real possibility. But there was Mike, who she was realizing again, looked better and better as a partner. It started with his devotion to her father. Only someone who was devoted to advancing the interests of James Duncan Stevens as she was could understand her devotion, no apologies or excuses necessary. Their common devotion provided an easy and natural topic of conversation they both could share.

There was the danger that it might become incestuous, though that was less threatening than the possibility of a chasm between them if only one were devoted. There was another advantage. They could discuss the most sensitive information without fear of compromise.

They were nestled together on Jim's chocolate colored leather couch, his only piece rising above the Ikea level, sipping Margaritas, munching chips and watching the local TV news. An update had just been delivered on the "puzzling" Stapleton case. Were the Russians involved as opposition leader Congressman Spurlock was alleging daily on the floor of the House?

"You talked to Klimov?"

Mike nodded as he licked a bit of salt from his wide rimmed glass.

"And . . . ?"

"He categorically denies his people had anything to do with it."

"You believed him?"

Unlike her father and Mike, her view of the Russians was less generous. Traces of older attitudes from the Cold War and the Putin era still infected some of her views. She didn't actively dispute her Dad and Mike-she kept doubts close at hand just in case-but her share of the general enthusiasm about the new Russia was considerably less. Trust but verify she said more than once.

"I did," Mike said without hesitation. "More importantly, your Dad does as well."

"I guess I'm not surprised," she said.

"Well, look at motive, he said putting on his forensic manner. "If you assume Kataev is sincere in wanting better relations, why do this? He knows what the impact would be. If the victim had been Russian, we might possibly have looked the other way, though even that's a stretch. But an American in DC? That's a double whammy. Only a stupid man would do such a thing. Kataev is not stupid."

"Doesn't rule out a Moscow rogue, some Moscow Spurlock who wants to undercut Kataev."

"True, and I asked Klimov that."

"He was equally categorical?"

"Not quite. But he was fairly certain a rogue is not at work."

"And you believe him?"

"I do. I think I know when a man is lying. Klimov was not lying. He says if a rogue's at work they will take care of it quickly." He paused to taste some more salt. "By the way, did you know he was a film director at one time at Mosfilm?"

"Klimov?"

"Yea, had a big reputation, so I'm told. We should look him up some time. I'm sure the Smithsonian would help."

"What's Mosfilm?"

"Russia's Hollywood. It's in Moscow, a kind of film city, like Cinecitta in Rome."

"So what's that prove?" she asked. It irritated her a bit when he came on like some kind of cultural maven. "Cinecitta?" she asked archly. "Aren't we showing off?"

He laughed. "Sorry, I forgot you went to UK under graduate and law school."

"You forgot the Rhode's Scholarship at Oxford," she said.

"Anyway, it proves he's an interesting man," he said. "And I didn't forget Oxford. How could I? You remind me of it so often."

"This the Margarita talking? Anyway, if he's so interesting why don't we invite him out to dinner. He married?"

"He is."

"A former Russian movie starlet?"

"Have no idea," he said. "Want another Margarita?"

CHAPTER SIX

ROUND TWO

The House was assembled for its weekly question session. The Prime Minister and members of the cabinet pertinent to the discussion sat at a long table below the speaker's dais facing the house members.

The Great Constitutional shift, as the recent government reforms were known, adopted the British practice of question period. It kept the government responsible to the House and forced it to publicly explain its policies and actions.

Leader of the opposition Congressman Spurlock led off.

"Mr. Prime Minister, has this government protested to the government of Russia the dastardly murder of an American citizen on American soil?"

"As the Congressman well knows, we have not. There is no proof that the government of Russia is involved in the death of John Stapleton."

"Most curious, Mr. Prime Minister. Is it not true that traces of the deadly Russian nerve agent Novichok were found on the body?"

"That is true, Mr. Spurlock. Traces of Novichok were found on John Stapleton's lips."

"And is it not true, sir, that Novichok is possessed only by the Russian government? We do not have Novichok in our chemical and biological arsenal. Is that not true, sir?"

Gilbert Spurlock came to prominence as a county prosecutor in western Kentucky, known for his dogged pursuit of quarry, large or small. He was known, not altogether warmly, among journalists, as Gilbert the

Hound. It was a reputation he carried proudly. He loved trotting out his forensic skills on the house floor whenever an opportunity appeared.

"It is true, Mr. Spurlock, that Novichok is a Russian nerve agent, and it is not found in our arsenal.

I'm curious to know what the conclusion our prosecuting attorney draws from these undeniable facts."

"That Russia is somehow involved in the death of this Mr. Stapleton."

"No other conclusion is possible?"

"I see none, sir."

"That vials of Novichok have somehow gotten on the black market and made their way into the hands of certain criminal or terrorist elements, these are not possibilities, sir?"

"How likely is that?"

"I don't know. But such is possible, is it not?"

"Not likely, in my view."

"Possibly not, but the government cannot be quite so cavalier. Before we haul the Russian government into the dock, as my eager friend would like, we owe it to good policy to make sure of our facts. We have raised the matter informally with the Russian government and they have categorically denied any involvement."

"As they would," Congressman Spurlock replied, a smirk in the direction of his cohorts on the right side of the legislative chambers. The Americrat Party and the Democrats, with whom they were in coalition, occupied the center and left sections of the fan shaped seating arrangements, left and right as the seats faced the speaker's dais.

"It seems to me, Mr. Speaker," the Prime Minister said, addressing the entire house and not just his interlocutor, "before making the matter public we owe it to ourselves and the Russians to first approach the matter privately. We have no proof other than the presence of Novichok that Russia has any involvement in this mater whatsoever. We have many substantial reasons to doubt they would be involved. As the gentleman from Kentucky is aware, we are currently involved in discussions with President Kataev's government to find ways of improving the relations between our two nations, relations that have been in a state of permanent discord ever since the lamentable regime of Vladimir Putin. President Kataev initiated negotiations and we have responded. Good relations are as much in our interests as in his. How likely is it he would do things to undermine his own policy? Highly doubtful. It is well understood the gentleman from Kentucky does not believe good relations with Russia are possible. On matters Russian, let me point out, he is about as well informed as he is about many another issue that has come before this house. How well that is I will leave to the judgement of the individual members. Despite his efforts, the government has every intention to continue engaging with President Kataev. We believe the public supports us."

"Perhaps it won't at the next election."

Jim Stevens laughed. "That remains to be seen. And it is three years off."

National elections were now held every five years. All national office holders stood for election at the same time, president, senators and house members. The aim was to encourage a more unitary and coherent expression of the public will than the previous split arrangements permitted.

CHAPTER SEVEN

JIM STEVENS

Jim Stevens views on Russia changed after a visit to Russia several years earlier. Before, he viewed the Soviet Union and its successor the Russian Federation as an aggressive power, intent first on communizing the world and failing that, undermining the West. It harassed the Baltic Republics for joining NATO and grabbed the Crime and invaded Ukraine's eastern provinces in retaliation for preferring closer economic relations with the EU than with Russia.

He read Tolstoy, Dostoevsky, Pushkin and Chekhov after his visit. Without denying any of the previous history, he believed that a people who produced such a literature had to be more than just the seed bed of brutal, authoritarian regimes. This was a literature equal to any, as was its music from composers the quality of Tchaikovsky, Stravinsky, Shostakovich and Prokofiev. They could easily stand with the Western canon. Russia was more than the primitive, authoritarian civilization it was often made out to be.

There were also its enormous sacrifices of blood and treasure suffered in defeating Hitler and helping save Western Europe. Jim believed there could be more to Russia than depicted in western propaganda.

Then along came Vasyli Kataev who saw Russia as part of the West and wanted to be its good neighbor. Talks began almost immediately.

The Rasputin Circle met for lunch twice a month. All four of its members, retired Foreign Service Officers, had served in the embassy in

Moscow. Their lunches were always at some English style pub in either Georgetown or Capitol Hill, the more English in atmosphere the better. Some of the members even favored British styles of dress-tweeds, overcoats with capes, even a deer stalker cap or two-a habit they claimed to have picked as a natural consequence of their years of cosmopolitan service abroad. Some would even have dropped a little British English into their speech if it hadn't sounded so affected. A deer stalker-those tweed caps with a bill front and back like Sherlock Holmes wore-might have passed as an amusing eccentricity or even the garb of an actual Englishman, but saying shed sual for schedule or al lew min ee um for aluminum was an affectation too far. None of them wanted to sound like a phony.

John Stapelton had been a member of the circle. The other four members were Paul Fordney, retired CIA and a former station chief in Moscow, Jim Pernick, Deputy chief of Mission-Charge- Anthony Schulick, economic counselor, and Fred O Brien counselor for press and cultural affairs. All of them had been in Moscow together, and all were united in the idea that few outside themselves really understood Russia. The corollary to that was any policy straying from their informed views was in error. They stood together in opposition to Stevens' Russian policy and voiced support for Congressman Spurlock's opposition. "The Russkies will eat Stevens' lunch," they all chortled in chorus.

On this Tuesday, their first meeting after Stapelton's body had been found, they discussed John's death.

"It shows how weak Kataev really is," Fred O Brien said. He was a mid-sized man with a full head of wavy, gray hair. He smoked a pipe and as cultural counselor of embassy wore a slightly academic air.

"Weak?" Schulick asked. He was short, dark and thin and what was left of his hair was shaved close to the skull, a slightly mid-eastern look. Behind his back his colleagues called him the Arab. As an economist among officers with a political orientation he often felt an outlier. His skeptical air was often just a device to buy time to absorb information or ideas new to him.

"Why would Kataev do this?" Jim Pernick asked rhetorically. He had been the embassy's second in command. "He wants to improve relations with us, so of course it's not Kataev. It's rogues from Russian intelligence, enemies of Kataev. I agree with Fred. Kataev is not totally in control.

As a former Deputy Chief of Mission-charge whenever the Ambassador was out of country-Pernick assumed position of first among these equals in their discussions and the last to render judgement.

He was also a world class name dropper, larding his conversations with "as Andrei was telling me the other night," or "when I was at the Kremlin, Vladimir mentioned," Andrei, and Vladimir names, of course, so obviously well-known their identity required no explanation.

Fred O Brien drew on his pipe and released a slow cloud of smoke. "Some people in the FSB aren't buying Kataev's Kumbaya line, Putin men."

"Like who?" Schulick asked glancing at Fordney. CIA. He knew the FSB better than anyone.

"Several possibilities," Pernick cut in, insisting on his prerogative. Boris Zaporozhets, Artem Tupolev and Gersh Chertok are good bets. "

"Efim Velsky, too "Fordney added.

Pernick nodded.

"One of them is behind this?" Schulick asked deferentially. Russian grain production, industrial output and energy generation were his fields of expertise.

"Likely," Fordney sad. "It would help to know for sure in fashioning a counter narrative against Stevens."

"I'll see what Langley can tell us," Fordney said

CHAPTER EIGHT

WHO IS JOHN STAPELTON?

Driving home from lunch, Paul Fordney recalled the first time he met John Stapelton. They were crossing the embassy grounds on their way to the chancery, the embassy offices. The row of embassy residences and guest quarters was behind them. The tall, lean man with an open, almost youthful face was a stranger. Since he was coming from the line of embassy residences and was carrying a brief case it was safe to assume he was on the embassy staff. There were no visitors as far as Paul was aware.

It had to be the embassy's new political counselor, John Stapelton who had just arrived. He had a lean figure and youthful, sympathetic face, intelligent, too. Paul immediately felt he wanted to get to know this man, and, he had to admit, get to like him.

On a sudden impulse he approached the tall figure and held out his hand.

"Paul Fordney," he said, "here with the embassy. I'm betting you're John Stapelton. They said you had arrived."

When introducing himself he usually said he was in the political section, the usual cover for CIA officers stationed in the embassy. But Stapelton, new head of the political section, would know that wasn't true.

Stapelton replied with a quick, friendly smile. "Yes, I know who you are. Glad to meet you. You've been here over a year now, I'm told? I look forward to comparing notes. My last assignment here was close to six years ago. I'm sure much has changed."

Paul was pleased this Stapelton did not instinctively fend him off as other embassy officers might have, protecting their purity against the dark doings of the CIA. Stapelton knew who he was and was unafraid.

As Paul crossed the Key Bridge in his suburban and made for the GW Parkway he felt all over again the tingle of those first moments. Turns out they had a lot in common.

Gilbert Spurlock's office kept up the pressure. Just about every other day a story leaked from the office of the leader of the opposition on the subject of the Stapelton murder. The media accepted this stream of news with open mouthed eagerness and begged for more.

"Russian Source for Novichok Strongly Suspected," stated one headline. "Stapelton Known to Have Been Thorn in Putin's Side," screamed another.

It was a copy of the Post with this headline that Prime Minister Stevens held in his hand as Mike entered his office. Mike understood immediately why he had been summoned.

"How much do we know about the unfortunate Mr. Stapelton?" the Prime Minister asked.

"Not as much as we should," Mike replied, "or as much as I should." Knowing such things was one of his responsibilities.

He called the Russian desk of the State Department to arrange a visit.

Mike preferred face to face to a phone call for serious business. Body language often told as much as verbal expression.

He felt an exhilaration walking through the atrium like lobby of State, flags of the worlds' nations displayed high overhead to suggest the elevated seriousness of the work being done on the floors above.

The office he was looking for was several stops up of the large elevator to which the guard at the check-in post directed him. Mike's prominently displayed ID was a door opener, winning immediate recognition by guards and a quick wave through security. He was spared the showy measures of protocol formerly given White House aides, no high ranking, nervously deferential members of the department there to lead him through the department's many layers.

Henry Good was found in the middle of a labyrinthian set of offices like some protected prize, subordinates and secretaries surrounding.

He was a thin, anxious looking man in his late thirties or early forties. He looked up quizzically as Mike entered unannounced. Mike politely knocked on the door fame to show he came as a colleague, not a superior expecting deference.

Mike always checked. Paul Good, he was told, spoke fluent Russian having served two tours in Russia as a political officer at the embassy in Moscow and the consulate in Petersburg.

To what do I owe the pleasure? Good said with a friendly smile. Mike was known in the bureaucracy as a collegial man who didn't stand on protocol. He wanted to get things done and would as soon drop by your office as summon you.

"Tell me about Stapelton," Mike said without preamble.

"You speak of the unfortunate, late John Stapelton, I presume," Good said.

"I do," Mike replied. "Tell me about him."

"Retired, as you probably know. Two tours in Moscow, the last as counselor of embassy for political affairs, in effect the third man in the embassy. He was also my boss."

"You were there at the time?"

"I was, his deputy."

"Good man to work for?"

"He was, at least by my lights."

"There were other lights?"

"John was demanding. He was good, and expected you to be on your mark. Maybe a little unfair since not all of us had his talents, but it made us work hard and do our best. But he was fair and understanding.

If you weren't a good fit, he'd quietly help you find another assignment without prejudice. I liked working for him. So did the rest of the section."

"Any possibilities that someone who was a bad fit left there carrying a grudge?"

"And who later got his revenge on John, you mean? "

Mike nodded. Any good investigator would have to consider the possibility.

"You're investigating his death?"

Mike was surprised at the question. Novichok, Prime Minister Stevens' demarche on Russia? Surely Paul Good should not be surprised.

"Why wouldn't we?"

"That there's an investigation, yeah, but why not the police rather than the Prime Minister's office?" He gave Mike a questioning look.

"The political sympathies of the DC administration are no secret. That the police, who might share those views, would glibly conclude that the presence of Novichok is proof enough that the Russians are involved, meaning the Kataev government, is disturbing. It is well known Governor Shaw does not share Prime Minister Stevens' views of President Kataev. Police might think the same thing. All this plays into Spurlock's hands, intentional or not."

"So much the worse for them," Good said with asperity. "We here at state know a damn sight better."

Mike was happy to hear that. "But it doesn't rule out some rogue Russia element, does it?"

Good shook his head. "No, but a rogue is not too likely either, though it can't be ruled out absolutely. If there is a rogue, he would most likely come from the FSB. Boris Zaporozhets, Artem Tupolev, Gersh Chertok, Efim Velsky would be the most likely candidates.

"Mike shook his head. Who are they?"

"All high ranking officers in the FSB, Putin acolytes. None of them are on board with Kataev's opening to the West. They would love to see Kataev and his opening to the West gone."

"So you think if one of them is involved, it's to embarrass Kataev?"

Good shook his head. "A possibility, but I'm not there yet. They'd be the most likely suspects, but I don't know if any of them would go that far. Kataev is a reformer, liberal, even, at least by Russian standards, but he's no patsy. You can mark him as one of Russia's iron fisted leaders. Mess with him and you're looking at hard time in a select Siberian rest camp. You'd have to be awfully sure of your protection to risk that. I don't see any of these guys taking that chance. Langley tends to agree."

But it's said by a few of the pundits, presumably with good connections here at State and Langley, that John Stapelton was a thorn in Putin's side. A motive for revenge? Was he a thorn?"

Good laughed as though reminded of an old joke. "We used to take bets on how much longer Putin would put up with John before declaring him PNG."

"Kicking him out? He was that good?"

"One way of putting it. Yeah, John was that good. His close contacts with Putin's opponents, even while their ranks were growing thinner and thinner, irritated Putin more than a little. He also kept a close eye on Baltic affairs, especially Estonian. He made several trips to Tallinn and was very interested in keeping Estonia and NATO close. All of that got back to Putin. We teased him about having a girlfriend in Tallinn, he went there so often. To get his ashes hauled, we joked behind his back."

"He had a girlfriend in Tallinn?" Mike asked. "Wasn't that dangerous?"

"No. He wasn't married. No need to hide it."

"He actually had a girlfriend there?"

"No one knew, and we didn't dare ask anyone in the embassy there. That would have gotten back to John, to our discomfort. He was somewhat secretive about his private life. Estonian women are said to be attractive, and John was a good looking man. But he wasn't someone who just let nature take her course. Far too self-disciplined for that."

None of which, Mike thought to himself, stopped John Stapelton from winding up at the foot of the statue of Alexander Hamilton with traces of deadly Novichok on his lips. "Anything else you can tell me about him that might help?"

"You know about the Rasputin Circle?"

"Rasputin, the mystical monk who had the ear of the Czarina? Killed for it wasn't he? "

"Seems you know at least something about Russian history."

"I was a history major. I took one survey course of Russian history. What is the Rasputin Circle?"

"A group of retired foreign service officers all of whom served in Moscow and who oppose Prime Minister Stevens' demarche with Russia. They frequently state their objections in the Post, principally Paul Fordney and Jim Pernick. I think Pernick had a piece in last week's Post calling Stevens' policy sadly misguided."

"Yes, I saw it. It was on our radar. I didn't know they were part of a group called the Rasputin Circle."

"It's not a formal name. Just a name they and their friends use among themselves."

"And how are they relevant?"

Paul Good smiled enigmatically, "John Stapelton was a member."

CHAPTER NINE

LOUISE AND MIKE GET ON

There were times when she wondered if she wasn't her father's daughter, would she even be there? Mike was as hard working as a stevedore and as focused as a laser with little time for anything but work. He fit his social life in when he could. Her proximity made their arrangement a natural; more, too, she hoped.

Their arrangement-if that's what it was-had just naturally fallen into place without much discussion.

She was living in Blair House, replacing her mother, dead these two years, covering the social parts of her father's life for the times a hostess was needed. The Blair House staff easily managed her father's domestic needs otherwise.

It became evident soon enough that few social occasions at Blair House required a hostess. Most events in which a hostess was required-Fourth of July, Thanksgiving, Christmas, state dinners for visiting heads of state and other important dignitaries-were held at the White House. Social occasions at Blair House by and large were working lunches, dinners or gatherings for drinks with congressmen or officials. The staff easily took care of these.

Her father let her know he'd understand if she wanted to strike out on her own. She might also have noticed, if she had been looking, the occasional hint her Dad dropped about Mike. He thought they fit.

Proximity and convenience would not have been enough on their own. She'd rather be by herself doing something interesting than with just anyone doing something boring. She thought Mike felt the same way.

Their personalities meshed like a pair of well-worn shoes. They were both interested in broadening their intellectual horizons. Washington was richly accommodating.

The Great Constitutional Reform, as many scholars and news media called it, simplified the lives of the prime minister's staff. They were no longer as consumed as members of the White House had been by the need to keep an immediate grip on the many strands of government activity. Now each cabinet assumed direct responsibility for a good deal of policy and execution, the prime minister and his modest staff exercising just general direction and supervision. The detailed work was done by the various cabinet staffs, all of whom had a direct interest in the success of the government.

Secretary of State Steve Brecken and his people were making all the arrangements for the visit of Russian Foreign Minister Smyrnov. Mike needed only make sure a weekend at Camp David was scheduled. Smyrnov, a nature lover, enjoyed woodsy rambles. Camp David's many winding trails amid acres of pine and oak forest were the perfect venue. The walks would give Stevens and his secretary of state plenty of time to get know Smyrnov.

Mike and Louise were enjoying the bite in the air of this crisp Fall evening as they walked hand in hand along one of Georgetown's deliberately charming brick sidewalks. They were going to a concert of music of Haydn and Mozart held in a converted 19th church. Its gray stone architecture and interior of plaster and wood made it a good choice for 18th century music played by a chamber orchestra.

There were three pieces on the bill, Hayden's Drum Roll Symphony, Mozart's piano concerto # 21 and his Overture to the Marriage of Figaro. The orchestra was of the size known to Haydn and Mozart and its instruments were authentic to the time. The strings were cat gut, not steel, and the valve less winds were of wood. The piano, piano/forte, was a reproduction of an instrument Mozart would have known, smaller than a grand with a tone and body of sound much lighter than its modern descendent.

"You haven't heard Haydn until you've heard him played by an orchestra on the instruments of his time," Mike said by way of preparation. Louise had done some reading. She had learned there were several ways the drum roll introducing Haydn's symphony could be played. Haydn left no instructions. Some played it softly, others more robustly.

She also learned original instrument groups sometimes played in a lusterless, academic way, relying on authenticity of sound-thinly toned cat gut strings, woodsy winds- to carry them. Sadly they sometimes missed the spirit of the work. "Sound but not music," as one critic put it.

She was ready to put the Georgetown Baroque to the test, a group organized by Gene Klemperer, a violinist in the National Symphony. The coupling of Mozart's Overture to the Marriage of Figaro with his Piano Concerto #21 was inspired. The opening softly thumping chords of the concerto harkened back to the low mutterings that begin the overture. The concerto's opening was quickly overtaken by a sprightly theme, happy and affirmation, which Mozart spins out in one delicate variation after another. The second movement's theme, singing, was accompanied by a thrumming accompaniment. Louise' lively imagination saw a meadow draped in early morning mist through which the piano came tripping, dreamy and light hearted.

After the applause died down Louise leaned over and said to Mike, "That middle movement would make such a neat movie theme."

He laughed.

"What's so funny," she asked, ready to be offended at his . . . condescension?

A movie did use it. I'll explain later. Let's get a drink.

The Haydn kept up the high, lively spirits spun out by Mozart. She was ready as Gene Klemperer lifted his baton and gave the down beat.

How would he play that drum roll?

The drums began as a low, distant thunder and then swelled to a moderate crescendo before receding in the distance. It sounded right to her. The rest of the piece was lively, inventive and never, never dull or lack luster. Haydn had lots to say and a happy time saying it.

The nave's Gothic feeling and the warmth and vibrancy given the music by the wooden pews made for a totally satisfying sonic evening. For Louise the nicest thing about ii- no electronics.

They walked down Wisconsin Avenue toward the Key Bridge enwrapped in a glow. The Metro stop was in Rosslyn across the river. Neither spoke.

At the middle of the bridge Mike stopped.

"Check out at the river for a minute? See how the reflected lights look like diamonds dancing on the black water.

She made to tease his poetic fancy, but held back. He was right, the dancing lights did look like sparkling diamonds.

Their view was upriver toward The Three Sisters, a set of large rocks in the middle of the Potomac. They marked the end of the river's navigable reach. Beyond were rapids, falls and rock strewn stretches of water all the way back to its West Virginia sources. It's what made the canal necessary.

"Georgetown did us a big favor," he said, "keeping the Metro out."

"How so?"

"If it had accepted the Metro stop, we wouldn't be making this walk. We'd be hustling to the Metro, forgetting the concert and these charming views."

"I'm with you on the views," she said, "but in winter? A cold wind off the river would make anyone forget a concert, no matter how good. Why didn't they put a Metro stop in Georgetown? The corner of Wisconsin and 20th Street would have been perfect. You could still take the bridge, if you wanted."

"It wasn't said out loud, but the feeling was, no riff raff from the Metro on their trendy little brick sidewalks. They wanted Georgetown for the Georgetownians."

"Snobs," she snorted. "May they be inundated by waves of drunk sailors. " After a pause, "I have a question."

"Mmmm?" he replied, turning to her.

"What's the movie that used that theme by Mozart?

"Elvira Madigan," he said.

"Never heard of it."

"Really? Thought you were doing some reading."

"I was. No mention of a movie. What kind of movie. About Mozart?"

"No. You're thinking of Amadeus."

"Never heard of that, either."

A career in the law and work for her father had dug for Louise a deep but narrow furrow of learning. Mike's background was much richer. It was one of his attractions."

"It's about . . . ". He paused, looking for a way to capsulize the movie's colorful and questionable speculations about the supposed musical competition between Mozart and Antonio Salieri, a rival court composer. Salieri, consumed by jealousy over Mozart's almost divine-like musical gifts, poisoned his more talented rival. Any synopsis would be too long and involved for the moment. The movie's biggest attraction was the page after page of Mozart' incomparable music it offered.

". . . never mind," he said. "I'll tell you about it another time. Elvira Madigan," he said, "is the tragic story of star crossed lovers. He's an aristocratic Danish cavalry officer. She's a commoner. Marriage between them is socially impossible. After struggling with their hopeless dilemma, they commit suicide. "

They used Mozart's sublime music for such a stupid story?" She was genuinely upset.

"Not everyone thinks it's so stupid. Romeo and Juliet?"

She snorted. "Also stupid. What if Elvira and her aristocratic cavalryman got married and then one of them died? Would the other commit suicide just to stay together?"

She laughed at the absurdity. "Maybe if both were old and near the end. But young, with a life ahead? What self-indulgence. And for what? Protest life's stupid absurdities?"

"So you say submit to your fate?"

"Unless you accept the consequences of opposing it, yeah. What else is there? So they marry. Now he is socially ostracized, cut off from family funds and friends, just one more commoner tending someone else's horses. She takes in washing. How romantic! If they're willing to endure all that for the sake of being together, then go for it. Otherwise, use your common sense. Suicide rules everything else out. It's not an answer."

That could go on until the river dried up. But he hadn't stopped there just to admire the view or indulge whatever philosophical discussion happened along. On the subway they'd be easily recognized-their pictures were often before the public-and people would strain to eaves drop. On the middle of the Key Bridge, with few pedestrians and nothing but a dark river consumed by its own romantic preoccupations, eaves dropping was not likely.

"I'm worried about the Smyrnov visit," he said, abruptly changing subject.

She laughed. "Join the crowd. It's on Dad's mind constantly.

Mike knew as much as anyone about the state of the Prime Minister's mind, except for Louise. Family closeness and intimacy was a garden of unguarded remarks not shared outside. Mike didn't mind.

"I know. The Stapelton murder is blocking everything. Smyrnov is coming to increase public support for the understanding between Kataev and your Dad toward. The Secretary of State is preparing a formal agreement to submit to Congress and the Russian Duma. The Stapelton mess throws a damp cloud over everything. We need to find out how and why he was killed. "

"You're saying it wasn't Novichok?"

"It may have been Novichok, but who used it and why? It's not Kataev, we're surer of it. But we need to prove it to shut Spurlock up. Until then, he has the floor".

CHAPTER TEN

JIM STEVENS, POLITICIAN

Gilbert Spurlock missed no opportunity to hang the Socialist tag around Jim Stevens' neck. Stevens hardly resisted. "The word Socialist," he pointed out, "had the word society at its root, and politics," he added, "is about society governing itself, deciding such important questions as how the community shares the wealth it creates. Is it only for those who control the spigot, or do all who helped create that wealth have a right to a fair share? Who decides? The market or the society?"

John D Rockefeller did not create the oil he exploited, nor did he drill for it, refine it or distribute it personally. Lots of other hands were involved. So why should he be the one to decide what share of that wealth is given to each? Why should it be up to him, just one man, no matter his contribution?

Jim's answer was, "a fair share for all with the government stepping in if the private sector could not do the job justly." The market didn't always have the best answer.

He gave a speech on the House floor calling on America to "understand itself as the community it really was rather than a collection of special interests occupying the same geographical space," the way Spurlock saw it.

"A true community," Jim said, "worked to insure the security and prosperity of all its members, what the Preamble to the US Constitution called the common good."

He used the military as illustration, a community that took care of the basics so its members could concentrate on their military duties. How good would a soldier be if he had to personally take care of his own training, housing and health care, regardless of personal circumstance? Too distracted to perform well?

It was a daring thing for an Americrat to do. "No," he said, anticipating Spurlock, "I am not suggesting we militarize our society. I am saying the military sets an example from which the society at large can profit, making sure all its members have the necessary health care, education, housing and retirement they need to be effective citizens. "

It was a question of practicality, not political ideology, Jim pointed out. A sick, poorly educated, poorly housed citizenry was not a productive citizenry; it wasn't even a happy one.

In the old days a heart problem called for an aspirin a day and easy on the stairs, something everyone could handle. Now a range of expensive therapies were available from stents to heart replacement, well beyond the average means.

"So what do we do," Jim asked, "treat only those who can afford it? Or spread the cost over the entire population so all can afford it?"

This was Jim's starting point. It governed all he did in politics: how could society do for industrial or modern man what the old agrarian society had done for the yeoman of old?

"But man is an individual, responsible for his own destiny," preached Spurlock. "Government has no business interfering."

"That worked in the 19th century," Jim replied. "It doesn't in the 21st."

What private enterprise cannot cover, government must.

This thinking brought Jim to the head of his party in Congress and finally the chair as prime minister, a job Spurlock wanted for himself. He never forgave Jim for denying him it.

Jim Stevens felt more comfortable amid the elegant 19th century comforts of Blair House. The more stately formalities of the White House and Oval Office were not his style.

He had deliberately chosen a spacious corner room overlooking leafy Lafayette Park and Andrew Jackson's equestrian statue on one side and the White House on the other. The row of Federalist period red brick town houses opposite, there almost from the birth of the city, contained an inspiring share of the Republic's history. The refuge of Dolly Madison's widowhood was almost opposite, and near it was the home of William Seward, Lincoln's secretary of state, where Lincoln often visited to relax and exchange political gossip.

Stevens saw himself as an ordinary citizen gifted with a few uncommon political talents and some charisma. But it had been hard work that helped him rise through the ranks to the leadership of the Americratic Party, from which point he became head of the government when his party won the most votes in the 20 elections.

Jim took to heart the aims of the government laid out in the preamble to the constitution: form a more perfect union, establish justice, insure domestic tranquility, provide for the common defense, promote the general welfare and secure the blessing of liberty. That was more than persiflage to Jim Stevens. "Nothing was said about the interests of party or particular interest groups as the objects of the government," Jim said. "It aimed to promote the interests of "We the People."

Most profiles called Jim Stevens a communitarian. It wasn't a name he used himself, but it fit. Yes, we are all individuals, he agreed, but none of us lives alone. We need each other and work best together.

He was proud of his role in giving life to the National Health Care and Retirement Act of 20 , guaranteeing every American full health care coverage from birth to death and a comfortable and adequate retirement at the end of their working life, all paid for by a national VAT.

When governor of Kentucky, he changed how the Blue Grass elected its Congressmen. In place of the old single member districts, usually offering just a narrow choice between two candidates, he instituted multiple member districts with rank ordered voting. Voters had a wider choice and more opportunities to elect the best supported candidates through first and second choice votes. The Blue Grass showed the way and the rest of the nation followed.

With that same spirit of community, Jim Stevens now approached Russia, the community this time the community of nations.

The world had changed a good deal since Jim entered politics. It was now sorted into three large economic and geopolitical blocks-Asia, Europe and the Americas. China dominated Asia though the US, through Japan and India, maintained a significant presence. Europe was dominated by the EU with Russia under Kataev edging closer and closer, recognizing itself as a western civilization. Its religion, after all, though orthodox, was Christian.

The US maintained a major interest in the old world, its spiritual homeland. It had gone to war twice to keep it free from domination by hostile interests.

The Americas-north and south-were a separate sphere, their economic and political ties closely entwined, US in the lead.

With their strong European connections Jim Stevens believed the US and Russia were natural partners in making the world community, most specifically the western part of it, a better place to live.

Gilbert Spurlock did not see it that way. He was a man of partisan motives and narrow vision. But for John Stapelton's murder, Gilbert Spurlock would have only a small platform from which to impede Prime Minister Stevens reach across the seas to President Kataev.

CHAPTER ELEVEN

THE RASPUTIN CIRCLE

Mike was passing Jackson's stature on Lafayette Square on his way to Blair House when his smart phone rang. It sounded urgent. He fished it out of his brief case. It was Detective Barody.

There's an interesting development in the Stapelton case you'll be wanting to hear.

"Great. What is it?" Mike asked, eager for anything to dispel the cloud darkening Stevens move toward Russia. Stapelton was affecting matters Russian in death far more than he had in life.

"Not over the phone," Barody said gruffly. "It's not secure. How soon can you get over here?"

Mike was wasn't sure how much of Barody's rebarbative manner was baked in police arrogance and how much was resentment carried over from the time DC was the step child of the federal government. The wiser course, Mike decided, was "to get" himself over to Barody's office as quickly as he could.

"I'll call you back in five," he said. "I'm walking now to Blair House. Need to check first with the Prime Minister."

"You can't call?" Barody asked dryly.

"No. Same reason you won't discuss this new development over the phone," Mike said. He tapped the off button.

The Blair House driver dropped Mike off in front of the police station on 23rd St. The station was two row houses converted to police use, the townhouse look to assure the neighborhood the police were just one more good neighbor. Police stations elsewhere in the city resembled fortresses.

Detective Barody was seated at his desk in his spare, utilitarian office. He got up to extend his hand when Mike walked in.

"News, you said."

"Yeah, puzzling news," the detective replied.

"Oh?" Mike said, his heart dropping just a little. He was half hoping to hear something like, 'we just caught the guy. He's not Russian.' Case solved, Spurlock thwarted. Puzzling didn't seem to suggest that.

"I see," he replied with reduced expectations.

"We just got the coroner's report."

"Yes?"

"Seems Mr. Stapelton died of a heart attack."

"Heart attack?" Mike asked, puzzled. "You mean induced by the Novichok?"

That wasn't much news. What difference did it make if the Novichok induced a heart attack, mortal nerve damage or liver failure? Dead was dead, Novichok the cause. It seems they were still at square one.

"No, not induced by Novichok," Detective Barody replied. "According to the coroner, Stapelton was dead from the heart attack before the Novichok was applied. It wasn't absorbed by the body."

"Did the coroner say how the heart attack occurred?"

"Bad heart. Enlarged, I think he said, a walking time bomb. Apparently anything could have set it off."

There was something a little guarded about the good detective's manner.

"So a heart attack means natural causes. We're not talking murder anymore?"

"So it would seem. Don't know if it's possible to induce a heart attack. If it was, I'm sure my ex-wife would have tried. Gave me ulcers, instead. Death by natural causes is what the coroner says. "

"And the Novichok," Mike replied, "how and why did that get there?"

Detective Barody smiled. "Sixty four dollar question, I guess," he replied. "As of now, no answer."

"And the coroner has no opinion?"

"Except to say it wasn't the Novichok that killed him, no. It had nothing to do with the death. Would have, if the heart hadn't gotten him first."

"Curious," Mike said for want of anything better.

Detective Barody grinned. "Yep, I say that a lot. "

"Is the coroner going to release a statement to that effect?"

That would dispel at least some of the mystery. The Russians could hardly be accused of inflicting a heart attack on their old enemy, John Stapelton. Yet the question remained, 'why the Novichok and by whom'?

"That's the funny part," the detective said.

He glanced at the door to make sure it was closed. A fear of eaves droppers? Something going on?

"Normally the coroner does make a public announcement, but up-stairs," a nod of his head toward the ceiling, "says to hold off. Until the Novichok question is settled, no public statements."

The beneficiary, Spurlock, Mike thought. As long as the case was open, it could be milked for attacks on Stevens. No wonder Detective Barody was being cautious. Columbia's governor and Spurlock were po-litical allies. It was no longer a police matter. Politics now governed.

This was why the detective was reluctant to talk over the open phone. *Somebody* could be listening. Detective Barody was doing him a big favor.

Mike gave him a look. "I get it," he said. "I won't forget." He shook the detectives hand with added warmth and turned to go.

"Well, I'm just a cop," the detective said, his voiced low. "I go where the facts take me. I'm too dumb for politics."

Mike waved as he left the office. You think? He said to himself

CHAPTER TWELVE

CONGRESSMAN SPURLOCK

"**D**on't matter, " Congressman Spurlock said. "Heart attack or not, Novichok was in the body. That means Russia. Nothing's changed."

With this, Congressman Gilbert Spurlock dismissed the report. It had been leaked to his office by the governor of Columbia, John Shaw, a political ally and colleague in opposition to Stevens. John Stapelton died of a heart attack, but there would be no public announcement to that effect. It was a favor to Congressman Spurlock.

As long as Novichok was part of the picture, Spurlock's opposition to Prime Minister Stevens remained viable. Novichok meant Russia, and its presence in the body of a dead American diplomat, a Putin enemy, screamed revenge. Let Stevens prove otherwise.

Partisanship was to Gilbert Spurlock as the public good was to Jim Stevens.

The old constitution permitted gerrymandering, suppression of opposition voters and the unlimited flow of cash in election campaigns. All this had made Spurlock's job easier.

That was gone now. Congressional elections were held in multi member districts which used rank order voting. Gerrymandering was no longer relevant. Private money was banished from elections by a constitutional provision making federal elections tax supported, modest individual contributions to candidates and parties excepted to encourage direct citizen participation. Limits were also placed on what could be spent on advertising related to a federal election, placing the integrity of elections above any distant threats to the first amendment.

The Supreme Court and lower federal courts no longer had jurisdiction over congressional legislation, except for alleged threats to the Bill of Rights. Challenges to legislation were to be made at the ballot box, not in the court house.

All this made Gilbert Spurlock something of a walking anachronism, his survival a matter of sentiment, inertia, and lack of an immediate alternative. Prescient observers understood his long range prospects were dim to nonexistent, but until a new party leader more adept at navigating the new political landscape emerged, Gilbert Spurlock was it. He was undisputed leader of the Republican opposition and he meant to take his old political antagonist down while he could.

The Senate was no longer a legislative body. The great constitutional reforms of 20 _ turned it into a senior governmental advisory council, there to assure bills passed by the House met real national needs rather than merely partisan ones, to identify areas of national need to be recommended to the house for legislative action, and to insure legislation conformed to the formal requirements of the constitution. The Supreme Court exercised judicial review only over acts by state legislatures.

States were organized into several regions, the number of senators from each region determined by its population. Category one regions got one senator; category two, three senators, and the highest category, five. Senate members had to be fifty years of age and recognized leaders in various field of public life, including private business, academia, government, medicine and the law. Members were elected to a term of five years by the region's voters. The quality of service, not partisan standing, was the criteria.

Spurlock's antagonism to Jim Stevens was years in the making, starting when Stevens was governor of Kentucky and Spurlock was speaker of the Kentucky house.

An old friend and political mentor of Stevens had died. Stevens wanted to give a state funeral for Thom Davis in honor for his years of distinguished legislative service to the Blue Grass. He was also a personal friend and the man as responsible as anyone for Jim Stevens' steady rise in Kentucky politics.

Spurlock refused to vote funds for a state funereal or allow Davis's body to lie in state in the capitol rotunda. As far as Gilbert Spurlock was concerned, Thom Davis's death was strictly a private matter. He meant this as a political defeat for Governor Stevens and a personal humiliation.

"Let me have a little talk with Mr. Spurlock," Mike said. He was as close as anyone to Jim Stevens, excepting his daughter. A former newspaper columnist, Mike had been with Jim Stevens since his days as mayor of Lexington.

"What good would that do?" the governor asked.

Mike told him.

The governor laughed. "Normally I'd say no, too personal. But Gil is playing dirty and getting personal himself. He's asking for it. Go ahead."

Mike had told the governor some years' earlier Gilbert Spurlock's daughter, Meredith, had an abortion. Nothing remarkable about that, abortion's legality being beyond dispute since a constitutional amendment definitively settled the matter. A fetus was part of a woman's body, beyond the reach of anyone but herself.

Gilbert Spurlock bought none of that. He was a publicly avowed Christian and a loud, frequent critic of abortion, "sin, pure and simple, contrary to God's law." He and his daughter Meredith offered frequent and loud witness against the godless practice, swearing it would never darken the door of their Christian home. Those who had recourse to it were sentenced to perdition

Gilbert Spurlock assumed Mike was coming to beg for a public funeral for Davis. He smiled, relishing the prospect of sending Stevens emissary home empty handed. Stevens presumptuously' occupied the office meant for Spurlock, if God's word had meant anything to those ignorant Kentucky voters.

"Well, to what do we owe the pleasure, Mr. Sullivan? We don't see you much in these parts."

"No sir, I stay on my side of town. However, I've come today on a matter of importance to the citizens of this commonwealth."

"You speak of a funereal for Mr. Davis, I presume?"

"I do, sir. It would seem his life of service to the commonwealth should be marked in some signal way. Surely, this should not be a partisan matter. As good Kentuckians why can't we unite in giving Mr. Davis a state funeral? If anyone deserves it, Thom Davis does. Many a commonwealth figure of less distinction than him have been accorded the privilege. The governor respectfully requests that Mr. Davis be given his due."

"He does, does he?" Spurlock said with a venom that was a toxic mix of mean spiritedness, vindictiveness and self-righteousness, unusual, even in political infighting.

Mike stood there, patiently waiting, looking at Spurlock.

Spurlock stared back. "I think we're done here," he said dismissively.

Mike took a breath. "I'm afraid not," he replied in a voice that said the fight was just beginning. "There's more. I do this reluctantly, but you leave me little choice. You remember Dr. Jerry D'iorio, Jerrold D'iorio of Louisville, the Satan of Abortions as you called him?

Spurlock's eyes narrowed and he gave Mike a thin, cold smile. "So were talking blackmail? You have to be joking. Is your boss really that stupid? People say he's a clever man. I wonder. Let me tell you, nobody threatens Gil Spurlock in this town. Doc D'iorio?" He laughed. "Doc D'iorio is dead. Use his name. I'll just deny it. People know me as a man of God's word. They'll take my word over yours any day. And they know my daughter too, a pillar of the church. So go ahead, play your little game. See what happens. D'iorio, indeed." He gave a dry laugh.

Mike returned the smile. "Church lady today your daughter might be, but back then she was just a frightened, seventeen year old girl with a problem-pregnant and no husband. She got an abortion and you approved it. We have the proof."

"No you don t. Those papers were destroyed at the time. My orders."

"Afraid not. Dr. D'iorio may be dead, but his nurse isn't. You remember her, Anne Greene, whose license you tried to revoke several years ago, your way of trying to take Dr. D'iorio down? And you remember who defended her, exposing your charges for the lies they were: Thom Davis. Anne is ready to testify Meredith had an abortion and you signed the approval form."

Spurlock waved his hand dismissively. "Just the word of a spiteful woman swearing revenge on me for standing up for the health of innocent woman against the abortion racquet. Trot her out. It won't matter." The smile this time was broader, but still hard and frosty.

"And what will your followers think when they see the consent form you signed, your name on it big as John Hancock's. What then?"

"You're bluffing. I said those papers were destroyed, on my orders."

Mike shook his head, a little smile of his own. "Afraid not," Mike said, enjoying himself. "Anne kept them. Didn't trust you."

He opened his brief case and slowly drew out the consent form and held it up for Spurlock to see. "Your signature, big as life. Makes you a self-serving hypocrite. I'm sure your followers would love to see this. Give them a different idea of their 'leader.' Might change their minds about some things."

He let that sink in.

"You really want to risk the reputation you've worked so hard to build, your image as God's faithful toiler in His vineyard, the image now sullied because his unwed daughter unfortunately got pregnant and had to have an abortion, with his express written consent? Little hard to explain that I'd say, you being such a man of God and all, one who forbids his followers to have an abortion but feels free to authorize one for his daughter. Makes you no better than those who supported Roe v Wade."

He paused to let Spurlock think about it

"You really want to go through all that, just to stiff Jim Stevens? Means he gets the last laugh. I thought you were smarter than that."

He stared at Spurlock, enjoying him squirm.

"There's an easy way out. All it takes is a state funereal for Thom Davis. That happens, this consent form goes away for good. Imagine the applause, one more generous, warm hearted act by Gilbert Spurlock to honor a Blue Grass hero.

"This is black mail."

Mike shrugged. "So?"

Spurlock's eyes shifted. The funereal was on.

Frankfurt said it was the largest funereal anyone had seen for some time. Thom Davis lay in state in the Capitol rotunda for two days with an honor guard drawn from Kentucky's National Guard units. The cortege taking him to his grave site had more shiny black cars in it than a new roll out from Cadillac. He was buried in a small cemetery on a knoll overlooking the city close to the monument marking Daniel Boone's final resting place.

Everyone said it was the grandest funeral they had ever seen.

Gilbert Spurlock swore he'd never forget it.

CHAPTER THIRTEEN

PUTTING OFF SMYRNOV

These thoughts were much on Gilbert Spurlock's mind as he rose to address the House this cool, overcast morning.

"Mr. Speaker, when will the government reveal the results of its investigation into Russian involvement in the tragic death of a John Stapelton, an American hero the Russians had every reason to want dead?"

The Rasputin Circle had been busy. Spurlock quoted from a recent editorial page piece in the Washington Post that detailed the heroic efforts of Embassy Political Counselor John Stapelton "to beard the criminal Putin regime in its own den, a regime only one step below infamous Stalin's in perfidy." The wisdom of warmer relations with a Russia that used murder to revenge itself on political enemies was questioned. "This government clearly does not understand Russia. The bear may have changed his coat, but it's still the same old bear."

"It seems the question the honorable member from Kentucky poses might best be kept for the question period this week," the speaker said.

"Under normal circumstances the speaker would be right. But I ask this house, with the impending visit of Comrade Smyrnov, the Russian Foreign Minister, in mind, do we have the luxury of waiting even one day before we have an answer? Can we spare that much time?"

"Spurlock's right about that," Jim Stevens said. "We either have an answer to Stapelton's death, or it might be best to postpone Smyrnov's visit until we do."

"How will Kataev see that?" Mike asked. "A sign we are softening?"

"Good question," the Prime Minister said. "Sounds like it's time for another chat with your friend Klimov."

The meeting was in the same tavern in Warrenton, Virginia, and followed the same MO: rented cars rather than official vehicles, casual dress as though out golfing at Warrenton's regionally famous golf course, the usual deception and concealment to throw media watchers off the track. Neither side wanted to risk suggesting a crises in Russian/ American relations.

Elam Klimov was already there seated at a corner table conveniently covered in shadows.

"I see you've changed barbers," Mike said as he sat down. "Less Moscow and more Washington now." Mike knew Elam was moderately vain about his appearance, something Mike enjoyed tweaking him about. It was a sign of the growing warmth between them.

"When in Rome," Elam said a bit sheepishly.

"It suits you," Mike said. "Makes you look even more Viking than before."

Certain Russians who shared Elam's well sculpted features and silky blond hair took pride in the look that bespoke descent from a certain Rus, mythical leader of Viking freebooters who once coursed up and down Russia's rivers as free-lance marauders.

Elam reddened with pleasure. "Well, you know what they say about good genes."

"Have you ordered?" Mike asked.

"Only drinks. I just got here. I ordered you a Manhattan made with Canadian Club, the way you like. I'm having a Martini. I didn't order any food. "

"Vodka Martini?"

"What else?" Elam replied. "I am Russian."

"So," Mike said after drinks arrived, "the question is . . . "

"Smyrnov visit . . ." Elam finished.

"Exactly. Would we be misunderstood if we suggested his visit await the resolution of the Stapelton case?"

"Depends on why. What is administration's latest thinking about Stapelton's death?"

The question hid just a hint of wariness. He and Mike were friends, something that gave him great personal pleasure, but they weren't family. Friendships between governments or nations often included discordant elements, occasionally embarrassing. Congressman Spurlock was more than proof of that.

"You are not blaming Russia?"

"Not at all," Mike assured him. "In fact I have some encouraging news to share on that score."

"Yes?"

"We know Stapelton did not die of Novichok. He died of a heart attack, and it was not induced by Novichok. That was put on his body after he died."

The relief on Elam's face was clear. "This is news. Will the Stevens' government make an announcement?"

"We will. But Spurlock will deny it and continue to accuse Russia of Stapelton's death."

Klimov thought for a moment. Then he grinned. "I might do the same, if I were Spurlock."

Mike shook his head. "Yea, but you're not Spurlock. You're better than him."

Klimov dipped his head, acknowledging the compliment.

"Until we know who and why the Novichok was put on Stapelton, we won't be able to shut Spurlock up."

"So, back to Smyrnov visit."

"Exactly. Our thinking is, postpone it until the question of Novichok is eliminated. Once that is done, Spurlock has nothing more than his petty annoyance against us. At that point a visit from Foreign Minister Smyrnov makes eminent sense. If he comes before, Spurlock will simply use the occasion to embarrass us and attack Smyrnov. Does neither of us any good."

"Agreed. Like here, there is opposition in Moscow to Kataev. At the moment they are quiet because he is popular. But they are ready to pounce at the first sign the West or US is playing Russia false. Spurlock's attacks are already causing rumblings. An attack on Smyrnov would make matters worse. "

"Just one of the down sides to democratic government," Mike sighed. "Until we have an answer, Spurlock will continue to make noise."

"The truth will set you free," Elam said with a laugh.

"Amen, brother."

Mike was certain the Rasputin Circle held at least one clue to that truth. He took the paper Paul Good gave with the names and phone numbers of the Rasputin Circle and called Jim Pernick.

CHAPTER FOURTEEN

WHAT THE RASPUTIN CIRCLE KNOWS

Jim Pernick agreed to meet Mike at a boutique sandwich shop in Old Town Alexandria, Pernick's suggestion. The shaded sidewalks and red brick town houses of Alexandria's old section had changed little since the days of George Washington and Robert E Lee, a look the city worked hard to preserve. It suggested neither giant was that far away.

It was a traditional, old fashioned sandwich shop that said tie dyed tee shirts and raggedy shorts were out of place. Jim Pernick was in the back, seated by a brightly curtained window. Mike had never met him before but quickly guessed the person in the slightly out of style gray tweed jacket was his man.

"Mr. Pernick," Mike said, extending his hand.

"Mr. Sullivan, I presume?"

"Indeed," Mike said and sat down.

Both ordered iced tea and something with guacamole, turkey, bacon and generous amounts of lettuce, tomato and bean sprouts on toasted whole grain.

"I'm puzzled by your invitation," Pernick said. "I'm sure you're a busy man. Can't imagine you're here just to discuss my latest editorial."

"Correct, though I would like to talk about it sometime. No, I have something more urgent in mind."

"At your service," Pernick said, folding his hands and giving Mike an expectant look, a posture he adopted at the embassy when faced with supplicants.

"I'm told you belong to a group called the Rasputin Circle?"

"I do, an informal group of old Russian hands. We get together once a month for lunch and discussion. Naturally, matters Russian are a staple of our conversations."

"So I gathered. John Stapelton was a member of your group?"

"Aha. I scent an agenda. Yes he was. A regrettable occurrence, John's murder. The Russians are responsible, of course. The Novichok proves it."

"That's what I wanted to talk about."

"Yes?"

You say it was the Russians?"

"Of course, who else?"

Obviously Pernick didn't know Stapelton died of a heart attack. Apparently the Rasputin and Spurlock Circles did not spin in neighboring orbits.

Mike decided to probe. "Why do you rule out other possibilities?"

"Are you serious? One word. Novichok. Who else uses that?"

"That we know of, no one. Unless some of it got on the black market."

Pernick snorted in derision. "You mean some American thug got hold of a little Novichok and decided to try it out on poor old John? The idea is absurd." He snorted again, a Harvard snort, not a red neck snort. Mike had looked up Pernick's bio. Harvard, class of 2010.

"But even if it was an American hand that applied the poison," Pernick went on. "It would have been at the direction of Russians. FSB would be my bet. Just out sourcing. Makes denial easier and avoids one more dead body from Novichok smeared with FSB finger prints. The FSB isn't all that sensitive about bad publicity, but a dead American on American soil by Russian hands might be a bit risky. Now, if John had been found in some back alley in SE Washington with his throat cut or a bullet in his head, we might think just a mugging gone wrong. But what mugger would have access to Novichok, or would use it in that way, if he had? And who else might want John dead? The Russians. End of story, or in this instance, case closed. "

He had the same smug look Spurlock had when challenging Mike to prove his daughter had an abortion.

"Why in your mind would the Russians want John Stapelton dead?"

Pernick had been Deputy Chief of Mission in Moscow. He might know something worth hearing. It was said he knew Russia well.

"John crossed Putin any number of ways. He was in close contact with Putin's political opponents. He gave them a voice in our councils and a measure of protection. Naturally, Putin was less than pleased. John also crossed swords with Putin over keeping Estonia a firm member of NATO. He let Putin know Tallinn was no longer the mouse in Russia' Baltic cat and mouse game. That gave Putin even greater heart burn. Keep in mind, Putin's former KGB. Actually, scratch that. There is no such thing as former KGB. Once KGB always KGB, and the one thing you need to know about the KGB is they punish any who cross them. Violence in all its sweet forms is their MO, including assassination. They don't forget. Skripel and Litvinenko prove that. The perfidy of these two ex-Russian intelligence operatives might have been in the distant past, but to Putin it was as yesterday."

"OK, I get that. But Putin's dead. A new man is in charge. Surely the FSB isn't pursuing the same old enmities contrary to Kataev's new course?"

"No, of course not. They couldn't get away with that. They'd be gone in an instant. But keep in mind, Putin the man is dead but the spirit of Putin is still very much alive and in insidious ways, and it is a spirit more in keeping with Russian history than the irenic platitudes of Kataev. People are wrong to think Kataev represents the real Russia. Kataev is Kerensky, Putin is Lenin."

Mike's cursory knowledge of Russian history just managed to get the analogy. Kerensky, the moderate head of the post Czarist provisional government, stood for liberal reforms democratically achieved; Lenin, his unrelenting opponent, stood for the dictatorship of the proletariat. Lenin won.

"So you're saying Kataev, like Kerensky, is doomed to failure?"

"That's putting it simply, if crudely, but yes, he is doomed to failure. Kataev is a westernizer. Russian will never be a western country. Its soul is an amalgam of Byzantine Christianity, Oriental autocracy and medieval peasant subservience. Western liberal ideas, in which your boss seems to put such stock, are simply a borrowed veneer. The real soul of Russia is symbolized by the sword and the icon, not rationalism and the rule of law. A strong central government and an overriding church are its two main pillars. Why do you think Putin made an ally of the Patriarch? He's aligned with those traditional Russian values. Kataev is not. You people don't get that."

"I defer to your knowledge of Russian history and your embassy experience. Perhaps you are right. Maybe the Russian soul is expressed by the ax and the icon, but does that mean Russia and the West are doomed to eternal enmity?"

"A legitimate question. Temporary agreements, at least, may be possible when mutual convenience requires. The cooperation during World War Two when we and the Russians were both in mortal danger is illustrative. But when the war was over, Russian history flowed back into the usual channels."

"Stalin? Had there been another leader, you're saying Russian history would still have run in the same course?"

"Another fair point. But Stalin was more Russia than Kataev is. And let me remind you, when the Cold War ended, long after Stalin was gone, Russia became Putin, not Gorbachev."

"Well, that raises all sorts of interesting questions. But they will have to wait for another time. Right now I have a more immediate concern. Russian involvement in the death of John Stapelton. You're convinced they are involved?"

"Definitely. I repeat, who else uses Novichok?"

"You're saying Kataev's government had a hand in this?"

Pernick shook his head slowly back and forth as though puzzled by Mike's "slowness."

"No, of course not. I'm no fan of Kataev, but he is not stupid. His desire for better relations with the West is sincere-misguided but sincere-and he won't do anything to jeopardize that. But he's paddling against the current of Russian history. The Russians may envy our technology, but they don't envy us. They think they're better than us, spiritually superior. They have suffered, we haven't, the revolution, the war and all that. They resent our material superiority and disdain us because it makes us soft. Russia can never be friends of the US the way Britain is. Prime Minister Stevens' policy is built on sand. It can't endure.

"So who then killed John Stapelton?"

"You want names?"

Mike was taken aback. "You're telling me you have names?"

"Of the usual suspects? Of course. Try Zaporozhets, Tupolev, Chertok and Velsky for starters."

"Yeah, Paul Good mentioned them, too. Senior members of the FSB and old Putin hands. You think they have gone rogue?"

"Gone? They always were. These guys are figures out of old Russian history. A fist in your face and fuck the West. The West is Russia's enemy-the French, British, German-they're all the same. They want Russia dead. Kataev is wrong. These guys want to put Putin back in the Kremlin, or at least his spirit."

Pernick's thesis had a narrow kind of logic. But was it the only thesis?

"Are you aware that John Stapelton died of a heart attack?"

Pernick tried to hide his surprise. "Heart attack? He said turning the matter over in his head. "I'm no expert on Novichok, but a bad heart? Wouldn't Novichok . . . ?" He shrugged.

"Induce a heart attack?"

Pernick nodded.

"I'm no expert, either, but the coroner says no. Stapelton had a bad heart. He died of that. The Novichok was applied later, after he died. None of it entered his body. Somebody was trying to make it look like Novichok killed him. But who and why? I was hoping you might have some insights."

Pernick looked thoughtful. "Well, even so, that doesn't mean the FSB wasn't involved. Let's just say they already had John in their grip, ready to apply the Novichok when his heart gave out. I can imagine the scene, pushing John in some alley, holding up the Novichok and saying, "This is from Vlad," their usual mix of politics and gangland. John's bad heart gives out and he collapses right in front of them. They apply the Novichok and then dump him in front of the Treasury, you know, in some kind of weird symbolic act, Hamilton, father of American capitalism and all that. Kataev is undermined and revenge is savored.

He looked at Mike, almost challenging him.

"And it is offensive that these barbarians can do this on our soil and our pusillanimous government does nothing. It's what happens when you play the Russians with a weak hand. A hard fist is what they need. "

"That's one scenario. There can be others, no?"

"You think?" Pernick said with the same tone he'd use with a subordinate who had just said something stupid.

"I do. The need is to find out what others."

CHAPTER FIFTEEN

DINNER WITH THE ENEMY

During the Cold War no one was invited to the home of a Soviet diplomat. The fall of Communism changed all that.

Elam's apartment was on the top floor of an apartment building on Wisconsin Avenue close to its intersection with Massachusetts Avenue. It was owned by the Russian embassy to house its diplomats. The National Cathedral was clearly visible. Mike imagined the discomfort the imposing view might once have caused the building's inhabitants.

But no longer. With the fall of Communism, the Russian Orthodox Church was restored to its honored place in Russian society. Putin routinely appeared in public with the Patriarch. When the Ukrainian Orthodox church split from the Russian Orthodox, Putin took it as a religious and national affront, and his involvement in the Syrian civil war was in part to protect Orthodox interests in that troubled country.

Mike didn't know what Elam's religious views were. His own sat ambiguously between agnosticism and atheism. He and Elam were parked in easy chairs enjoying the view of the National Cathedral's softly lit Gothic facade floating in a dark, velvety sky and the Russian Embassy's compound, visible several blocks away on Wisconsin Avenue, awash in harsh security lights. Elam's wife, Nora Mikhailovna, was off showing Louise the apartment.

"Wouldn't this window have been curtained before?" Mike teased.

Elam laughed. "Because of the view?"

Mike nodded.

"I don't know. Would depend on how secure the occupant felt and on how closely watched he might have been. A surprising number of people back then, including government and party officials, retained some religious feelings. After the death of Stalin and the reforms of Khrushchev, people were able to attend orthodox services once again without risk, and plays and Opera with religious themes forbidden before were again permitted. The Party, though, remained atheist.

"When I was a university student in Leningrad, I attended a performance of the oratorio Joan of Arc by the French composer Arthur Honegger. Before the performance, a party apparatchik came out to instruct the audience about the religious text of the oratorio which, he pointed out, was a dangerous piece of Western religious propaganda. It was the music they were there to hear.

"I had a friend in the orchestra and after I asked him after about the lecture. It's the price we had to pay to put on the piece, he shrugged. Now no explanation is needed."

"Are you a believer, Elam?"

"No," he said quickly, "but I am attracted by some of the dramatic elements of the Russian Orthodoxy services, the operatic rituals, the music, the priest's vestments, the icons. But I don't believe in God."

"So what meaning then do all these icons and rites have if there is no God?"

"You have to understand, before I joined MID, I was a film director. Drama and costume are in my blood."

"MID?"

"Ministerstvo Inostrannykh Del, the Ministry of Foreign Affairs."

"OK, I get the drama and costume, but the rest, the dogma, doesn't that make you uncomfortable?"

"No. Maybe I'm too Russian, but you have to understand it isn't easy making a film about Russian life without stumbling across the Orthodox Church in one way or another. It is too deeply woven into our culture. Not even Stalin could eradicate it."

"But apart from the rite and the vestments, you'd say religion is largely a collection of myths?"

Mike's own disbelief was based on a negative: there was no need for a God to explain the universe. Elam the same?

"No, it's more than childish myths. At heart, religion is simply a metaphor to explain things man had a hard time explaining otherwise. Science was primitive back in man's early history. Most natural mysteries were beyond man's ken. Religion supplied an explanation.

"Now science has replaced God with the Big Bang, and the sun has replaced the earth as the center of the universe, the earth once thought to be the center because Jesus lived and died there. Now we see things like The Virgin Birth and the Resurrection as metaphoric markers in the life of an exceptional man. And I could go on."

"So why religion, now that we have science?"

"Reasonable question. Even though we don't need it any longer to explain much of the world, man still clings to it for any number of reasons.

"It works as a poetic truth, God, the symbol of all those natural forces that so affect our lives, things like gravity or the laws of thermal dynamics, not to mention all the biological laws that govern us. But they're abstractions. We're more comfortable with stories and we tend to see things in anthropomorphic terms, God as a super human creating the universe, Adam and Eve the first humans, Moses and the Ten Commandments, Jesus on the Cross, stories more easily understood than scientific abstractions. Try explaining gravity in a way that would lead man to feel all warm and fuzzy and want to worship it.

"We don't dismiss the Iliad just because it's a mythic depiction of the Trojan War, if ever there was such a thing. And even if there was, nobody would take Homer as a documentarian. Yet we believe in the Iliad.

"And just because God is dead, so to speak, is no reason to throw the concept out entirely. God represents all those abstract laws of nature that move our universe just as the flag symbolizes so much about a nation. We know there is no Santa Claus-we call him Father Frost in Russia-but the figure represents an admirable aspect of the human spirit. It works on one level."

"Jesus, Elam, have you ever thought of defecting? We could really use you on this side of the Atlantic."

They both laughed.

"Actually," Elam said, "I always thought religion began with the first man to experience a thunder storm. Imagine him soaked by that torrent of water, deafened by those ear splitting peals of thunder and blinded by those flashing bolts of lightning that just turned a nearby tree into a column of cinders. A big, dangerous force that could well do him in. He needed to find a way to placate it so he would be spared. Thus sacrifices and religious rites.

"And remember, even those who accept the Big Bang see something appealing in Michelangelo's God creating man with a touch of his finger."

CHAPTER SIXTEEN

JOHN STAPELTON

The right honorable gentleman from Kentucky rose to ask the Prime Minister to explain why the government was postponing the visit the Russian Foreign Minister, Maximus Smyrnov.

"Is this a postponement or a cancellation?" Congressman Spurlock asked. "Does this mean the government is reconsidering its sadly mistaken belief that Russia and the US can be friends?"

Stevens replied. "It suggests no such thing, as I am sure the Honorable member must know. He is simply using the postponement of the foreign minister's visit to continue his ill-informed, partisan attacks on the government. I am amused to think that if we deemed President Kataev a threat to world order, Congressman Spurlock would be shouting how sadly misinformed we were about this angel of peace. Foreign Minister Smyrnov's visit is meant to make final arrangements on our proposed treaty of friendship with Russia. It's awkward to do this while the Congressman persists in creating a hostile climate by exploiting the unfortunate death of John Stapelton. As the honorable member from Kentucky is fully aware, Mr. Spurlock died of a heart attack, not Novichok. The Novichok was applied after he died, evidently in an attempt to sow discord between this government and President Kataev's. The Russian government had nothing to do with Mr. Stapelton's death. The matter is being investigated and we will report to the House when we have definitive information."

"Which I wish we did," the Prime Minister said with a dash of wry as he looked at Mike. They were in the PM's office, both regarding Jackson on his horse. Maybe he had an answer.

"Devoutly to be wished," Mike said apologetically. He fully felt the Prime Minister's desire to get on with things, settle the Stapelton business and get the Russian train running full steam.

"Possible rogues from the FSB is the best I can do so far" Mike said. "I'm not satisfied with that. There has to be another answer. If we just knew where the Novichok came from, we might find who put it on Stapelton. The why might then follow."

"You trust the police? Governor Shaw is not our friend."

"In this instance I do. The case is being handled by a Detective Barody. He doesn't seem to think much of our Russian policy, but he's an honest cop who follows the facts, not the politics. He can be helpful. In any case, he's what we have. Ask for a change and Shaw's people will just stiff us. The FBI can't get involved because Spurlock was a private citizen, making it a local matter. If he had still been in the Department, it could be a different issue."

He told Jim about his talk with Pernick.

"Not surprised he doesn't like my Russian policy," Stevens said evenly. "What is it about those people with Russian experience makes them think no one but they understand Russia? I grant them the benefit of their background, but that isn't a guarantee they're right. Knowing Russia is only half the equation. And what's this Axe and Icon all about?"

Mike tried to explain as best he could, the axe as tool and weapon and Byzantine Christianity as foundation blocks of Russian history.

"Is that so different from our own frontier experience and our individualistic and protesting version of Christianity. Makes us considerably different from Catholic Europe, yet we still work comfortably with it. Don't you just love how these intellectual theories tie up messy histories into neat, easily discussed packages? I'm sure the axe and the icon had something to do with the Russia we see today, just as the musket and the six gun played a role in our culture. I can see how Byzantine Christianity might have colored Russia's view of the Roman Catholic

West. After all, the two split over theological differences way back when. So that's a factor, but is it an insurmountable obstacle? The theorists may think so, but the pragmatic politician interested in building things rather than freezing them as they are, can't. And we can assume Kataev knows at least as much about Russia as this . . . "

"Pernick."

". . . does? I'll go with his instincts. We have a chance to repair a breach that has endured since the Russian Revolution. How responsible would we be if we just tossed that off because the experts say it is counter historical? With proper safeguards we could be on the verge of something new and historic. No statesman worth his salt would just walk away from that on the advice of the experts. Gil Spurlock might, but not Jim Stevens.   Let the experts be the ones who change."

Mike no more wanted media snoopers to know he was meeting with Detective Barody than he wanted them to know whenever he and Elam Klimov sat down to chat. Barody mentioned McDonald's on M Street near the invisible border between Georgetown and DC. It had been a while since Mike had gone fast food. Louise was an ardent champion of a healthy diet. She would indulge a hot dog at the ball park because that's what one did at a ball park, but otherwise fast food was off the menu.

Mike got there first and ordered a Big Mac meal, medium. He was just unwrapping the Big Mac when Detective Barody walked in. He waved to Mike as he ordered.

"So," he said to Mike as he sat down with his own Big Mac meal, the large variety. Mike wondered how the good detective stayed so rail thin.

"What's up?"

"Want to eat first, then talk?" Mike asked.

Barody gave him a puzzled look. "What, the federal government can't eat and talk at the same time? Tell me what's going on."

Mike laughed. "OK," he said, "so much for good manners."

Detective Barody grunted and took a bite. "I'm on a short break," he said. "So tell me."

"How helpful can you be in tracing this Novichok?"

Very helpful, Detective Barody said, Novichok is a dangerous substance. Somebody deliberately left it in a public place, endangering the public, not to mention a couple of policemen. Good thing we were wearing latex gloves. That increases my motive to find out who did it and, as the saying goes, bring him to justice. The interest is both professional and personal. "

"You're looking into it, then?"

"Just starting to. Stapelton's now on the back burner. Dying of a heart attack is not a crime. Dumping a dead body in a public space is, and so is reckless and dangerous handling of a hazardous substance. But as crimes go, they're relatively small fish. Leadership says look into it, but not as the expense of more important cases."

"You're slow walking it then?"

"Trying not to while looking busy else wise. One reason meeting here is a better idea than at the station. No curious eyes checking us out. Who would think we'd be meeting at a McDonalds to plot?"

They both laughed.

"I asked the Pentagon if they could help. But you know them, they're better at fighting world wars than at looking into little stuff like this. Takes 'em forever. But there is another possibility."

"Oh?"

"Know what Fort Detrick is?"

"Of course. The Army's chemical and biological warfare research center." Mike thought for a moment. "Damn! You're right. If the US had any Novichok, that would be the place. Why didn't I think of that?"

"Cause you're not a detective, for one thing."

"Yea, still . . ."

"So I'm asking the Pentagon if they have any Novichok at Fort Detrick. But, like I said, you know them. When it comes to this secret stuff, they're tighter than a new coat of paint. I got friends in the Maryland State Police and the Frederick police force. I'll be giving them a call soon."

"Well, you're way ahead of me."

"Wouldn't be, we work together."

"I'm for that. One reason I wanted to talk. We need to clear up this business of Stapelton's death. We and the Russians are close, but we can't take the next big step as long as Spurlock keeps claiming Russia is behind Spurlock's death. A treaty of friendship with a nation that murders American citizens on US soil? Not hardly."

"I get that. I'll do what I can to help."

"I appreciate that." Mike said. "But I can't help wondering why you're doing this? I know you're good man and a good cop and in the short time we've been acquainted I've grown to like you and to trust you. You're a straight shooter and you don't play games. But I gather you're not a fan of my boss's lean toward Russia and your governor likes it even less. So I gotta ask, why are you doing this? I know it's not my baby blues, and I do know you could be risking your career. Shaw is not a forgiving man. So why . . . ?"

Detective Barody grinned. "Jeez, long speech. Yea, okay, I like you, too. You aren't one of those government assholes who comes on all arrogant and self-important, and I don't trust the Russkies as much as your boss seems to. Before I was a cop, I was in the army. MP. Some of the old attitudes linger. But this is way above my pay grade, so I have to think he knows more than I do. I try not to let politics interfere. For all I know he's right. I've seen crooks go straight after they were brought up short, so why not Russia?"

"I appreciate that," Mike said.

"And, another thing. I don't really like political assholes telling me how to do my job. But one thing," the detective said.

"What's that?"

"This has to stay quiet, me and you working together. Nobody's to know except the few who have a need to know. I'll watch your back, you watch mine.

"Done," Mike said, "in a heartbeat."

CHAPTER SEVENTEEN

FRIENDS

From the diary of Paul Fordney: We're planning a vacation, John and me. From the first it was clear we could be friends. We're the only two bachelors on the country team. Everybody else, the DCM, political and economic counselors, public affairs, admin are all married. That makes it easier for them to socialize. John and I are the odd men out, difficult fits for many intimate social occasions. John once suggested maybe we should get married. That way we'd be invited to more dinners and parties. We both laughed. It was a **joke**.

He was sensitive and immediately understood where I sat in the embassy structure. It is never announced, even internally, who is station chief in Moscow. There are ears everywhere. Of course, in the country team setting it is hard to hide identity, and in any case no real need. Everyone has top secret clearance, and all understand the need for complete discretion, even those who don't have a high regard for what we do in the agency. I'm thinking of that elitist smart ass, Fred O Brien, the Press and Cultural Attaché. He thinks because he knows the names of all the major ballerinas at the Bolshoi he is somehow superior. But even he knows better than to reveal my identity. If he did, he would be on the next plane.

John instinctively knew to avoid, skirt around or not ask too much detail about certain topics. Even so, it is easier to talk with John because we share an interest in certain subjects.

Putin's political opponents, for one. (We both refer to the president for life as Vladi. We both find him an amusing, pretentious little prick strutting around like some punk pretending he can punch above his weight. He's just a jumped up mid-level KGB apparatchik with an uncanny knack for latching onto money guys, balloons that lifted him from a Leningrad functionary to a seat in the Kremlin and then the presidency. John and I were both keeping close track on the majors among Putin's political opposition, guys like Navalny, Kolobov, Popov and Malinovsk. There were a few details I couldn't share with John, names of a few people in opposition circles who were my informants. John respected that and never probed. Other than that, we were completely open with each other and shared a lot, to our mutual benefit.

Unlike some of our colleagues in the embassy (O Brien, again) and among Russian expert circles in the states (I'm thinking of you, George Gurov, and you Greg Miller and Jack Klutch and the rest of you wimps) we don' believe the bear acts the way he does because of mistreatment by the West or because we extended NATO to the Baltic states, threatening Petersburg. If we could just understand how badly Russia has been treated by the West, they simper (Napoleon, Hitler, McCarthy all trotted out here) and see things from Moscow's perspective instead of from that of an antagonistic US, peace would descend in a dreamy summer cloud.

John and I both know what they can do with their fucking peace. The Russian symbol is the bear for a reason, the same reason Putin rather than Navalny or one of these other guys succeeded Yeltsin. The bear is not a pet and he is not user friendly. Bears are omnivorous and will make a meal of you as soon as look at you. Both John and I understand that. It was one of the first things that drew us together and gave us a clearer understanding of Putin's moves (Vladi) and helped us keep the embassy from going off the deep end in some of its recommendations to Washington. Putin is an aggressive little prick who thinks the sun rises and sets in Moscow and who wants you to believe that shiv in his hand is an olive branch. Hah! John and I were onto him.

Our personalities meshed. He is laid back, sharp minded, wryly humorous and non-confrontational, pretty much the opposite of me. They say opposites attract, and maybe it is true. One thing, John and I never had to explain ourselves to each other. Each of us knew who we were and respected that in each other.

So this is how the vacation to Salzburg came about. John was in my office (we both routinely sneak up and down the embassy's inner stair case; the elevator is too public) to visit each other's offices. We really did have a lot to talk about. We also enjoyed being together, a feeling that grew on us slowly like soft moss on a giant forest tree. (Please excuse the poetic flight. It's just that I get so tired of all that bureaucratic prose I have to pump out.)

I asked John if he had plans for the summer. After a Moscow winter, summer comes as a deliverance. You greet it with open arms and take full advantage.

"I'm going to throw some things in the car and drive through Poland to Salzburg, Austria."

"Wow," I said, "that sounds terrific."

John looked at me. "Yeah? So why not come, too? We'll have a blast."

"You serious?" For some odd reason my heart was beating faster.

"Yeah, I'm serious. Come on. We'll have fun, and maybe you'll learn something," one of those dry little digs he throws in once and while. (Yea, I did learn something, too. Never knew much about Mozart until we got to Salzburg. Almost as if John planned it that way. But that was John, like an onion, the more you peel him the better he gets.)

I knew a lot about Russia and the Second World War (they call it The Great Patriotic War; tells you something about them) and explained as we drove west through Byelorussia how the few scattered villages and open spaces helped the Russia Army outflank German defensive positions, forcing them to full back, each retrograde move taking them one step closer to the old Vaterland.

There were few stone villages for the Germans to use as defensive positions. Once the Russians had wheels, including the endless stream of Studebaker trucks we sent them, they were able to exploit the open country. Victor, one of the embassy drivers, loves showing me around Moscow when driving me to appointments. His dad was in the war. They called the Studebaker Karol Darogi, king of the road. Nothing stropped it. Makes me proud to be an American.

The opposite happed to the Germans in the Bulge. They tried to flank our thinly held position in the Ardennes. But there were too many steams with bridges that could be blown and too many villages our troops could turn into defensive fortresses. They slowed the Germans down until reinforcements could arrive to squeeze the German flanks and halt their advance.

John listened to all this intently.

His turn came in Salzburg. John, it turns out, is a Mozart expert. (Expert is my word, not his)

We trooped through the apartment where Mozart lived with his family as a child, saw the statue of Papageno in a little square devoted to him-the bird man from Mozart's Magic Flute-and heard several concerts of Mozart's music. Turns out a Mozart music festival was on, two weeks of almost nothing but Mozart-symphonies, opera, all that stuff. They do it every year. It's why John wanted to be there just then. He hadn't told me that. Probably afraid I would turn him down. He might have been right. But now, after hearing Mozart, I would do it again.

Salzburg is certainly a charming town, all those Baroque buildings like architectural chiffon, surrounded by Alps and perched prettily on the fast rushing Salz River. Who wouldn't want to grow up in a place like that?

Not Mozart, according to John. He found it confining and wanted a bigger place where he could stretch his talents. Vienna was that place. One problem, John said over coffee mit slag-coffee with whipped cream-at a café on the mountain frowning down on Salzburg. We were sitting at an outdoor table. Mozart was part of the Prince Arch Bishop's court and needed his permission to relocate. The arch bishop said no. Mozart told him to go fuck himself and moved anyway. Sounds like my kind of guy, and his music's not bad either.

It's instructive that you can't get that far from Russia in this part of Europe. In the castle on that mountain-called the Festung, or fortress-there is a huge block of black granite inscribed with the names of every member of the local SS regiment killed on the Russian front. Odd to think of these scattered bits of Salzburg spread around Mother Russia like some toxic manure.

On our next to last day, John and I were walking along the Salz River across from the city. We happened to pass the Russian consulate. Standing on the river bank looking over at the city was a youngish man, clearly Russian by his dress and demeanor. John addressed him in Russian. His Russian is really good. Best in the embassy, some say.

"What do you think about Salzburg?" John asked. The Russians laughed. "Eta igrushka," he said. It's a toy.

Yeah, that's the Russians; childishly charming or at your throat.

NORA AND LOUISE GO TO A CONCERT

Mike was watching the late news when Louise returned form a concert at the Kennedy Center Terrace Theater. She had been invited by Nora Klimov to a concert of music by the Russian composer Scriabin performed by a Russian pianist.

She had not known much about classical music before Washington. Blue Grass had been her default mode when it came to music. It worked well enough in Lexington and Frankfurt and was even serviceable in the DC area with its pockets of Blue Grass fans and bars where good Blue Grass could be heard.

But Washington quickly taught her there was more to music than Bill Monroe. She happily expanded her horizons. The Haydn and Mozart concert had been part of the expansion.

"So, good concert?" Mike asked, looking up.

"It was, though there was a lot I didn't really understand. This Scriabin had a lot of things going on besides music. He was a theosophist."

"Theo . . . ?"

"Theosophist, Greek for knowledge of God. Nora explained it to me over coffee before the concert. A kind of mysticism that says we discover the deeper spiritual mysteries through meditation and revelation. He weaves this into his music, according to Nora. I didn't get that, though some of it did sound dreamy. She also said he believed there was a relationship between certain musical keys and colors. He saw D major as golden brown. "

"You saw golden brown during the concert?" he asked with a laugh.

"No, of course not."

She laughed, too. It did sound odd.

"But you know we do say things like he's in a blue funk, or she's green with envy, so is it really so bizarre to think D major is golden brown? Nora told me she attended a concert of his piano works in Moscow once. They projected colors on a screen to match certain moods of the music. She said it was quite effective. Anyway, I like it she's always on about something new or exciting. Can you imagine anyone in Lexington dragging me to a concert of Scriabin's music and then going on about theosophy and musical keys and color? I have to say I love it. I'm glad she invited me."

"I did notice how you two were getting along that night we were at Elam's."

"I like her. She's a smart lady and knows a lot of things I don't, about art, I mean. Did you know she's a gifted amateur pianist? She played a little for me that night while you two were talking. She plays beautifully. She says she could have had a professional career but she wasn't good enough to be more than middle of the pack, though she stands out as an amateur. But the real reason, she's also a successful actress. That's how they met, on the set of a film. She told me she gives invitational poetry readings here at the embassy for Russian speaking Americans. A lot of students of Russian attend. We should go some time."

"I'm up for that. Bet you Dad would be, too. Even the politics of it works."

"What I'm getting from all this is Russia is such a complicated place. During the Cold War and Putin era we demonized Russia-totalitarianism, repression of civil rights, lack of freedom and creativity, poor living standards. Yet we have people like Nora, as cultured and vibrant a person as any of us. How?"

"I suppose if you could answer that you could also explain the association of a monster like Stalin with such exalted spirits as

Prokofiev, Shostakovich, Khachaturian, Oistrakh, Richter, Gilels and Rostropovich. Wow! That old Cold War propaganda could be misleading. One of the things your Dad is trying to untangle. "

CHAPTER EIGHTEEN

THE RASPUTINS MEET AGAIN

John Stapelton was finally buried, his body released to the family by the coroner after keeping it several weeks for an official investigation.

The family wanted to bury him in Arlington National Cemetery. He had served two tours as a naval intelligence officer and considered making it a career before the state department beckoned.

But there were no more ground burial plots left. All burials were now in small crypts in a long marble wall, cremated ashes only. Instead the family decided on a well shaded cemetery in Great Falls, Virginia. Copses of tall oaks and pines seemed appropriate for a man who had sent much of his life in the exalted reaches of diplomacy.

The Rasputins attended as a group. After a brief appearance at the family's funereal home reception, the group repaired to a small tavern near Great Falls for its own observances.

At Jim Pernick's suggestion they ordered vodka to toast their departed friend, chilled, the way John liked it.

Pernick raised his glass. "To our fallen comrade, a casualty in the war against oppression. He died defending us."

"Hear, hear," they drank.

"We still certain Putin's people are responsible?" Fred O'Brien asked. As counselor for cultural affairs, he spoke with confidence about Russian music, theater, literature and art. Politics was another matter.

He was also knowledgeable about the Russian dissident artists of the Khrushchev and Brezhnev eras. But he knew little about the FSB except that its predecessor, the KGB, had harassed the dissident artists in the 1970s. It had closed down one of their exhibitions in a public park by dousing the participants with trucks used to water the park's plants.

"As certain as anything could be," Pernick said. "Who else uses Novichok? Does anyone else even have it?"

"I suspect we have it," Paul Fordney said, "at Fort Detrick. But who except the people at Detrick would have access to it? Those people are heavily vetted. We can rule that out."

"So it's the FSB?" O'Brien said.

"Who else?" Pernick said. "They have Novichok and they had a motive. John crossed them."

"Expect you're right," O'Brien said. "A terrible way for John to go. And what is our government doing about it? Making peace with John's murderers! Shameful!"

"Exactly," Pernick said.

He didn't tell O'Brien Stapelton died of a heart attack. It was inconsequential in any case. The Novichok was there, placed by FSB rogues. That John's heart gave out first was immaterial. He died while those FSB bastards stood by and coldly watched. O'Brien didn't need to know everything. He was a cultural type. Information shared was information diminished.

"Fred's right," Anthony Schulick said. "We can assume the FSB is behind this. No one else does things like that. The important question now is, what is our fucking government going to do about it? We can't let this stand. Yet what else can we expect from this lefty crowd? Kiss Russia's ass and we will have peace."

"You think the assassins are still in the country?" O'Brien asked.

"Doubt it," Fordney said. "Probably back in Moscow congratulating themselves."

"And if they aren't?"

"You worried?" Fordney asked with barely suppressed amusement.

"Well, some of us could still be vulnerable. We were all with John in Moscow. Why not any one of us as well? You're not worried?"

Fordney shrugged.

"Really?"

Fordney shrugged again.

Well if *you* aren't worried," O'Brien said, I guess the rest of us . . . I mean you Langley guys . . ."

"Maybe there's no danger," Schulick said, "but does anybody see a connection between this leftist government and the old communist state in Russia? Communism, socialism, the same thing. The government owns everything, letting you keep only as much of your hard earned money as it wants. Kataev might not be a Communist, but he's no raging capitalist, either. They have state run health care, state run airlines, state run everything. And Stevens wants that here? Over my dead body."

"Even so we're well on our way," Fordney said. "Stevens' national health care and retirement system. . .? It killed the private health insurance industry and private retirement plans are almost a thing of the past. Now they want to do the same to public transportation. Rationalization, they call it. Bullshit! It's expropriation, pure and simple! Well, over my dead body as well.

Nobody said it, but they all thought it, there already was a casualty to the Stevens' regime-John Stapelton. Schulick raised his glass, a second shot of vodka. "To a martyr," he intoned.

Mike picked up on the second ring. The call identifier said Barody. "News?"

"Just keeping you up to date," he said. "Pentagon says they don't discuss activities at Fort Detrick unless there's a direct order. Official police interest does not qualify. Seems to me they could at least say, yea, we got some Novichok for research, but they won't even say that. Frankly, I'd be surprised if they didn't. Be almost dereliction of duty not to. Still, not a word. Can you help?"

"I think so. Let me get back to you. This a good phone to reach you? Barody could be using a phone not traceable to him.

"Yea. It's my smart phone. It's good anytime.

He asked the PM if he had five.

"I do."

Mike explained the problem. Without hesitation the Prime Minister had a call put through to the Defense Department. "It's the Prime Minister," he said. "I need to speak to the Secretary. Fine. I'll wait."

He looked at Mike. We need to get this solved. Smyrnov won't stay on hold forever. We owe him some consideration." He held up his hand to keep Mike from responding.

"Greg? Yea, Jim. There's a little matter I hope you can be helpful with. It concerns the Stapelton case". There was a pause. "Yea, that's the one. As you remember, traces of Novichok were found on the body. What's that? No, no, it wasn't the cause of death. Heart attack. Yea, yea, that's right. The thinking here is somebody put it there to implicate the Russians. Yea, that's right. For obvious reasons. To stop that it would help if we knew where the Novichok came from. Could help in finding out who used it. Yea, exactly. So here's the deal. A Detective Barody from the Met police is investigating the case. Right B a r o d y. He's run into a stone wall with your people. No, no, I understand. Extremely sensitive. But it would be very helpful to us if he could talk to the appropriate people at Fort Detrick and anybody else over there you think might be helpful."

He listened for several long seconds. "Good. Thanks. 'Preciate it. I'll let him know."

He turned to Mike, thumbs up, and wrote something on a note pad, tore it off and handed it to Mike. "Have Detective Barody call that number to set up an appointment at Fort Detrick. They'll take care of the rest.

CHAPTER NINETEEN

THE NATIONAL PAST TIME, END OF SEASON

Louise knew as much about baseball as Mike. She would have said more, but that meant a fight. The good part was her arm didn't need twisting to see a game and Mike didn't need time to explain things. It was baseball fan talk the moment they entered National Stadium.

One difference, Louise was all aboard with little ball, moving the runner along by stealing, taking the extra base, hit and run, bunt, one hit at a time. It spread the excitement over several plays rather than just one big home run moment. Mike said he favored little ball, too, but he also hankered occasionally after the three run inning-two on and a homer.

For the moment it was their most serious disagreement.

As they entered the park heading for their seats Mike recalled the first time he saw a major league game. It was at Camden Yards in Baltimore, the home park of the Baltimore Orioles. He was about ten or eleven, early June. They were on a family vacation and the Orioles were playing the Chicago White Sox. His dad decided it was time Mike saw his first major league game. Mike played outfield for his Little League team in Lexington.

He remembered most his first glimpse of the field under the lights, the intense green of the infield grass, the glowing white of the Orioles uniforms and the vivid black and orange of their caps, colors operatic in drama and intensity, though at that age he had no idea what that meant. He didn't remember who won the game, but he never forgot that first, vivid look.

It was just fifteen minutes from play "ball," time to get beer and hot dogs. Louise got two dogs, one with mustard and the other with relish, temporarily abandoning her dietary scruples. She would enjoy her dereliction to the fullest sinful moment. The beer helped.

The Nats were playing the St. Louis Cardinals.

The first two innings, the teams felt each other out, pitchers testing their stuff. Both teams were little ball practitioners, manufacturing runs any way possible, not depending on the long ball. They put a premium on hitters who could handle the bat under any circumstance, delivering whatever the situation demanded-bunt, ground ball, fly to the outfield, anything to advance a runner or bring one home. Hitters who could bunt with dexterity or hit the holes in the infield were as valued as those who could go yard, hitters who either hit one out or struck out. That was one dimensional baseball.

The Nats started things off in the third. The batter, second baseman Dick Foxx, noticed the third baseman, who didn't have exceptional speed, playing relatively deep. Foxx swung at the first pitch, deliberately punching it foul. He wanted to take their minds off a possible bunt. The third baseman relaxed just a bit. Foxx thought the next pitch would be on the plate. The pitcher wanted to get ahead two and 0.

Louise leaned over. "Bunt," she whispered. Mike nodded. She had been studying Foxx. She knew he was a good bunter. She liked the way he was playing it, faking hitting away and then dropping the perfect bunt, all of it every bit as exciting as a home run. That took just one swing of the bat, then you just watched as the hitter circled the bases, not terribly stimulating. She preferred the little orgasms of pleasure one after another rather than one big one from a single swing of the bat.

Louise had it right. Foxx got an inside pitch that caught enough of the plate. He dropped it down the third base line, just hard enough to get past the pitcher but not hard enough for the third baseman to swoop in and throw before Foxx was past first base, a big grin on his face.

"Man on," Louise said smugly, "and the ball never left the infield."

The next batter, Seth Williams, first baseman, drove the ball through the hole into right field. Foxx rounded second headed for third. Only a strong throw would get him. The right fielder's arm was a cannon but not terribly accurate. The throw was on time but off line on the left field side. Foxx slid in easily. The next batter, Thompson, right fielder and left handed batter, took two pitches and drove the third deep to the second baseman's first base side. Foxx scampered home easily. Williams took second.

The next sequence was typical Nats little ball. Williams, not a particularly fast base runner but a smart one, jiggled up and down the base path as though threatening to steal. The pitcher was distracted and let his third pitch catch more of the plate than he wanted. Blair, a good bat handler, put a level swing on the pitch and drove it to right center. The throw was cut off to keep Blair to a single. Williams made it home with the Nats second run. The next two batters flied out.

"Two runs, manufactured," Louise said with a shudder of pleasure. "We're on our way."

The two teams were changing sides.

"What's this detective, Barody, that's his name? What's he up to? Getting anywhere?" Louise, like everyone else in the Prime Minister's office, was anxious to keep their Russian policy moving in the right direction. Stapelton remained an obstacle.

"Talking to the people at Fort Detrick in Frederick, Maryland. Said he'd call me after."

"Think he'll find anything?"

Mike shrugged. "I'm sure Detrick has Novichok. What that means I don't know. Maybe Barody will after he talks to them. He says cop work is like turning over a bunch of rocks to see what scuttles out. The trick is finding the right rocks."

The game remained tight. St. Louis scored a run in the fifth on a solo homer. The Nats pitcher was keeping the Cardinals off the bases, limiting the damage of the homer. But it did reduce their lead to one run. The Nats got the run back in the seventh on a combination hit, stolen base and a double down the left field line. The Nats held on and the closer, Chatsworth, shut the Cards down in the ninth.

Mike and Louise left the park smiling and went home to make sweet love.

Later, Louise got up for a snack from the fridge. She sat in the dimly lit kitchen looking out the window of the eighth floor apartment at the Anacostia River several blocks away. She felt good about how things were going between them. Mike might have been one of those self-absorbed jerks who thought of nothing but his career, leaving little time for a private life, romance just a sterile parade of one night stands.

But this was Washington and things would change. Her father wouldn't be prime minister forever. What then? She and Mike would need to find new work. She could always retreat to her old law firm in Lexington. They'd be thrilled to have her back. With her experience in government and Washington contacts? She would be golden. The memories of Lexington, though, were losing some of their luster now that she knew Washington. Could she really go back? If not, it wouldn't be that hard to join a good firm in Washington. Again the contacts and experience.

And Mike? Even more than her, he was firmly bound to Washington. On the upside, he'd have no trouble finding a new politician to work for if her dad retired, something he thought about from time to time. He was sixty eight now and could easily assume the mantle of elder statesman. Mike could stay with him but the challenges would be diminished. Would that be enough for him? And if each of them was pulled in different directions, away from Washington? What then?

CHAPTER TWENTY

BARODY HAS SOMETHING, BUT WHAT?

"We're upscaling?" Mike asked. This time it was a Paneras on H Street.

Detective Barody shrugged. "Thought I'd pander to your tastes this time."

Mike laughed. "Well, Detective . . ."

Detective Barody cut him off. "Ralph, it's Ralph," he said.

"Thanks," Mike said, "and I'm Mike. So, find anything in Frederick?"

"Yea, something interesting, but I'm not sure what it means, if anything."

"We advance by inches, not yards."

"The guy in charge of Novichok and other foreign nerve agents is named Zviad Tabidze."

"Georgian, as in Caucasus, not American South?" Mike asked.

"So I'm told."

Mike shook his head. "Sounds like someone is writing a movie script."

"You think? He has a cover story because he was extracted, that's how they describe it, from Russia a few years ago. His real story is interesting enough. He was educated at Moscow University and worked for the Red Army's biological warfare unit. All this is classified."

"It would have to be. I almost think you're kidding."

"I wish."

"And he was wearing a big sign that said PRIME SUSPECT? "

Ralph laughed. "Cool your jets, it's not that easy. I raised the issue with the Pentagon's Provost Marshall's office. They know all about his background. He was hired in part because of it. No question about his loyalty. He was thoroughly vetted and everyone's aware he'd be the go-to suspect in any case involving Novichok. The Pentagon checked him as soon as the Stapelton case broke. He's clean."

"Yea, let's not make this easy."

"I'm with you. Still, he might be a piece of the puzzle. All we gotta do is show there's a connection between him and somebody who knew Stapelton."

Mike lit up. "That gives me an idea. I think I have some rocks you can look under."

"Yeah?"

Mike told him about the Rasputin Circle. "Stapelton was a member. These guys all served in Moscow at one time or another."

Ralph smiled. "Worth a look."

"I've got their phone numbers at my desk. Can I text them to you?"

"That'll be great. It could be a lead."

"It's still too easy," Mike said doubtfully. "It's almost as if someone is dropping hints deliberately as a false clues."

"You're thinking movies. But you're right. It's all a little too obvious. Still, I've learned over the years not to overlook anything that looks even remotely connected."

"You have more patience than I do. I'm glad you're working this."

Ralph laughed. "It's not always that easy. Reminds me of a Gilbert & Sullivan song I used to sing. It goes, 'Oh, when constabulary duty's to be done, a policeman's lot is not a happy one."

"The Pirates of Penzance!" Mike blurted out. A few near tables looked over.

"You know it? Ralph said, surprised

"Yeah, I'm a big Gilbert and Sullivan fan. My favorite song is 'I've got them on a list.'"

Ralph looked at him blankly.

"From the Mikado? The Lord High Executioner, people he doesn't like, 'I've got them on a list, they'll none of them be missed.' My favorite is about chatter boxes on crowded trains who won't shut up. They're condemned "to listen to sermons by mystical Germans who preach from eleven to four.""

Ralph laughed.

"How'd you know the Pirates of Penzance?"

"I sang in high school. We put that on one year."

Mike looked at him, shook his head and laughed. "God, who would have guessed? So that's why you became a cop?" He laughed again. The idea was funny.

"Nah that was the army. They decided I'd be a better cop than a ground pounder. They were right, too. I liked being an MP. There was just something about catching assholes and putting them away. Still feels good."

"Sounds like you should be voting Americrat," Mike said, only half teasing.

"I don't know, cops, you know, are pretty conservative, law 'n order, family values, no wild stuff . . . But you know, your guy's got me to thinking."

"How's that?" Mike asked.

"Well, you know all this stuff about community, the common good. Cops know instinctively that a healthy community is a community without much crime. Now the poor neighborhoods, you see, there's crime there because people get pissed off they see people up on the avenues living the life and they're just scraping by, sometimes with nothing but welfare. Some of our cops come from neighborhoods like that. They know what a close thing it is between dealing drugs and keeping your nose clean. Sometimes we feel like zoo keepers, you know, hired by the rest of society to keep the animals in their cages. It can get to you. I think your guy is right, we have to be a community. Doesn't mean we all have to be the same, but it should mean no body is left behind. I mean, look, nobody in SE Washington asked to be born poor, no real chance at an education or an easy way out. And they know many of those stiffs on the avenue are there because they were born into families with a few coins to rub together. Now in the army we all had clothes to wear, food, place to live, health care. Army figured, provide that, we all did our jobs better. Is that so fucking hard for those people in Congress to figure out? How come the army knows it and they don t?"

"How come indeed?" Mike said. "How'd you like to meet the Prime Minister some day?"

"Yeah? He a good listener? Sure, why not?"

CHAPTER TWENTY ONE

TWO RETIREMENTS

From the diary of Paul Fordney: It was my decision to retire in Moscow rather than return to Washington, the way most do. I only half admitted to myself I wanted to stay in Moscow as long as possible because of John. If I had fully grasped that truth, I might have blurted it out at some inopportune moment when asked why retire in Moscow, not Washington. What was between John and me was our business alone.

And what were all those feelings between us, feelings neither of us openly acknowledged nor defined? Defining them would have laid it out for all to see. Also, defining means limits. It's better to feel than to clarify. Once you clarify, where's the ability to deny, if necessary? We were both experienced and (I can say it in the privacy of my own diary) expert bureaucrats. We knew enough not to paint ourselves into a corner. Leave open the possibility for more than one explanation.

Truth is, though, if it had been London or Paris, safe towns, I might have settled there for a year or two after retirement just to be near John. There was nobody in Washington.

But an ex station chief living privately in Moscow? No way. The rule of law, as the West knows it, doesn't exist in Moscow. Without diplomatic immunity, which I lose on retirement, I'd be as safe in Moscow as a lamb amid a pack of wolves. The FSB could strike whenever it wanted. The first Russian spy picked up in Washington or New York? I'm looking at a guest suite in the Lubyanka.

John and I talked about how we'd get together after I retired. He'd be back in Washington from time to time for consultations, and we talked in general terms about meeting in Europe for vacations together.

When I boarded the plane at Sheremetyevo for the last time, John came out with me, his diplomatic ID his pass to accompany me to the departure lounge. We didn't talk much. I wasn't sure what it all really meant. Neither of us is comfortable talking about our emotions. Was John escorting me because he was told by the ambassador to give me some kind of embassy send off? Or was he there for his own reasons, because he wanted to be there?

I couldn't ask, but how I would have loved to hear, "I'm here because of you, to show what you mean to me." As it was, we just chatted as we would have seated in the secure room for a country meeting, waiting for the ambassador to show up and begin. When John walked me up to the boarding gate, he embraced me (a man hug) and said, "You'll be missed," and walked briskly off. As he walked with his back to me, I thought I saw him wipe his face with the back of his right hand. Tears? God! How good would that be?

The next couple of months drained much of my emotional energy finding a place to live (a nice rancher in McLean, close to the agency but close to green country, too) and settling into my new life.

John and I exchanged frequent emails. It's a convenient but also limiting means of communication. You need to be a bit careful what you say in emails since they are not fully secure. Letters, snail mail, are much safer. But if I had written him a letter with not much more than the usual email chit chat, he might have thought it a bit odd. If I wrote what was really in my heart, he'd have only two choices: reciprocate my feelings or turn me off.

Then one day I got an email that changed everything. John was retiring, too, and, happy days, in Washington, as I had done!! There was nothing particularly odd or suggestive about that. Many Foreign Service officers retire to the Washington area-DC, Virginia or Maryland-because the Foreign Service had become more our world than Biloxi, or Springfield, or wherever USA, we started from.

John said he was offered another overseas assignment (DCM Poland) but it didn't interest him. He was hanging it up and, like me, settling down in Washington. He had no real family left in Beverly, Mass, where he had grown up. All the people he was closest to now lived in the DC area. Most important of all, he said, he looked forward to adding more chapters to our book.

I know there's another reason John wants to be in Washington. He doesn't talk about it, but I know it' there, hovering in the back of his mind. He wants to be ambassador to Moscow. The best place to make that happen is Washington.

Book was the word John used to describe us. He has his own way of putting things. What word would I have used? Book covers a lot of ground.

That we will both be living in Washington opens a long, bright vista. I can't wait to see what chapters we will write in our book. My imaginings have already begun. Some of them make me shiver.

Mike made it a point to touch base with Elam at least every several days. The Prime Minister was anxious to keep Moscow fully informed about developments in Washington, otherwise baseless doubts and suspicions might spring up like poisonous mushrooms in a damp Russian forest.

Mike took a sip of the drink Elam had ordered for him prior to his arrival. It was good Scotch, not vodka. Mike noticed that Elam's glass was also filled with Scotch, at least the light amber colored fluid swishing around his ice cubes didn't resemble vodka.

Mike tweaked him about it. "No vodka? What will Moscow say? "

Elam laughed, as he was meant to. "There are a lot of things you guys don't know about Russians," he replied. "Everybody thinks we drink nothing but vodka. Juri Andropov drank Scotch, Johnny Walker Black. They say he drank a bottle a day. His liver must have looked like a piece of old shoe leather. "

"Juri Andropov?"

"Head of the KGB in the late eighties. He became General Secretary of the Party just before Gorbachev. Drinking that way, he didn't last long. Cirrhosis, as you might imagine."

Mike knew heavy drinking caused severe health problems in Russia. But it wasn't something he wanted to dwell on. There were other things about Russian life he wanted to hear about.

On that night at Elam' apartment he had talked about his views on religion. Mike wanted to hear the same kind of talk about Russia.

"Are you familiar with the Axe and the Icon?" he asked.

"The book by Mr. James Billings, who used to be director of the Kennan Institute of Russian Studies? Of course, every Russian diplomat trained for the embassy here has to read it."

"And? What did you think?"

"We Russians have our own version of exceptionalism and don't think most Westerners understand us very well. Many in the West think we're just another western nation, though one retarded by Czarism and distorted by Communism.

"We are part of the West but not in the same way that France, Britain, Germany are, or the U.S.

We're Christian, but our Christianity comes from Byzantium, not Rome. Royal absolutism and serfdom persisted much longer in Russia than they did in the West with all the consequent political effects. Lenin defeated Kerensky in large part because Russians are more accustomed to rule by the will of one man than by rule by law and elected committees.

"Russia has often referred to itself as the Third Rome. The First was Jerusalem, the Second, Constantinople and the Third is Moscow. We see ourselves as the true descendants of the Byzantine Church, that is true Christianity. That colors how we look at the place of the West in the moral universe.

"Russians speak a Slavic language, not a Latinate or Germanic one. It's true, Poland and the Czech and Slovak Republics speak a Slavonic language as well, but they are Roman Catholic Christians and very much a part of the West. To the extent that language has an impact on the way one thinks, Russia is set apart from the Germanic and Latinate West.

"But these are differences, not barriers, and the differences are ones of nuance and emphases, not of kind. I saw the American film of Pasternak' Doctor Zhivago. I know the book well and could easily follow the story as the film tells it. But a Russian Doctor Zhivago would have been different in feel and nuance, just as a Russian version of Huckleberry Finn would have been. We'd see the relationship of Jim the runaway slave and Huckleberry, what you might call poor white trash, through a different colored lens."

"So you're saying Billing's book is off the mark?"

"For Russians, probably. But for Americans? The axe as tool and weapon and Byzantine Christianity certainly played a role in our culture, and if the book helps outsiders understand Russia better, all to the good. But we Russians think you'd get as much from reading Tolstoy, Dostoevsky, Pushkin, Lermontov, Gogol, Chekhov and Solzhenitsyn.

"In any case why should cultural and historic differences mean undying enmity? The French drink wine and the Germans drink beer; still, the EU happened.

"President Kataev and Prime Minister Stevens believe Russians and America don't have to be alike to get along. National differences and sensitivities have to be taken into account, but is that something we can't do? It doesn't take much to act like an enemy or make war. Much the opposite.

"Putin did not make things easy. Instead of putting Russia on a new path, he tried to recreate the glories of the USSR, unaffordable though they were. Nor is a background in the KGB the best preparation to be leader of a society groping its way toward a more liberal politics.

"Shredding the treaty that gave Crimea to the Ukraine in return for its nuclear arsenal, and then wantonly violating Ukrainian sovereignty because it wanted closer relations with the EU is the KGB way, not the way of rational statesmanship. What's the gain for Russia in antagonizing the US and the West? Because it's what the Soviet Union did? We need to change.

"Putin's politics were not in Russia's long term interests, unless your aim is to restore the old Soviet Union, neither possible nor desirable. Our best long term interests lie in developing our economy beyond the energy sector and cultivating better relations with the West, China and the rest of the world.

"It's encouraging Prime Minister Stevens wants to help us do that. What would it be like if Congressman Spurlock were the prime minister?"

CHAPTER TWENTY TWO

THE BOOK ADDS CHAPTERS.

From the diary of Paul Fordney: I gave John some space to settle in before suggesting ways of adding pages to our book.

I met him at the airport and took him to his town house on Capitol Hill, vacated by his tenant a month earlier. John's property agent had John's furniture brought from storage and set up for his arrival.

John invited me in for a drink. It was a very superior single malt Scotch. "I had my property agent lay in a supply of booze," he said. "I hate living out of a suit case."

He swept his arm to indicate the entire ground floor of the town house. "Everything I need to resume life here is already in place, groceries, kitchen equipment, furniture. As soon as I'm over jet lag, I'll be ready to go. I can't tell you how much I've looked forward to this moment, sitting here with you sharing a drink, nothing but time in front of us. Glorious."

And it was glorious. We both enjoy a good meal and we quickly established a lineup of restaurants we visited frequently. One favorite was an Afghan restaurant near the Duke Ellington Bridge over Rock Creek. The National Mosque was a block away. The sight of its slender minaret lifting delicately above the leafy trees of Rock Creek Park and the restaurant with its savory kabobs and richly colored rugs gave us a bit of the exotic we were missing now that we were back in Washington.

One day John called and said he was off to the National Gallery, one of his Washington haunts. Would I like to go? It didn't surprise me that he liked to hang out in art museums. His Capitol Hill townhouse showed what good taste he had, unlike his apartment at the embassy in Moscow, embassy furniture in the generic Scandinavian mode. It gave no indication of his personal taste apart from a few small personal items he brought in his air freight

His town house was pure John: leather chairs and a couch in various shades of warm brown and tan, richly colored oriental rugs on the velvety polished wood of his hard wood floors, art on the walls, some of it obviously original, and a kitchen full of pots and pans that would make a good French kitchen proud. John lived well. He was a bachelor and he could afford it.

So I wasn't surprised to hear he liked going to art museums.

"Look at the way Cezanne leaves little unpainted spaces in this portrait of his wife," John would say as though we had just stumbled on some undiscovered treasure. "It's characteristic of him. He makes the little bits of bare canvas do the work of applied paint."

We moved over to a Cezanne landscape, a painting of the butt end of a mountain, the dominant feature of the landscape, the colors flat and just a bit dusty, the way they might have looked in real life.

"That's Mount St. Victoire, John said. "It's just outside Aix-en-Provence, Cezanne' hometown, where he spent the last part of his life. He roamed the country side in search of subjects. Mount St. Victoire was a favorite. I spent several days in Aix a couple of years ago driving all around that mountain trying to see how he took a subject and made it his own. It's the difference between painting and photography. The photograph gives you the image itself. The painting gives you the soul of the thing as seen by the artist, the way clouds float over it, how shifting light mottles the landscape and modulates colors, how composition showing full mountain or just one part of it among its surroundings establishes a narrative.

Two paintings over was a still life, pieces of fruit resting on a patterned rug on a table. The fruit-apples-seemed to have real volume and heft.

"Makes me want to grab one and take a bite," I said.

John playfully wagged his finger. "Uh, uh, not advisable." His sense of humor was dry.

Our art rambles were usually followed by lunch at some interesting place with a slightly foreign air, of which Washington, with a fairly large foreign population, has several. As two gents in the retirement mode, we would talk aimlessly and at leisure about our morning. During one of these rambles John looked at me and said, "I'm really getting into this retirement thing. Makes me wonder why I didn't sooner?"

"You could have?"

"I had twenty some years in and was fifty before the Moscow assignment."

By law military and Foreign Service officers with twenty years can retire with full pension at fifty. Keeps the military from having too many overage colonels. The Foreign Service copied that, but with less reason.

"I could have pulled the plug then. But I wanted the Moscow assignment. He gave me a look I'll always treasure. "And, he said, "his face softening, "had I retired, we wouldn't have met. Think of that. "

"Certainly my loss," I said, stifling the urge to reach across the table and touch his hand, not yet completely sure how it would be taken.

I got my chance to play guide on a visit to the Civil War battlefield at Chancellorsville, some seventy miles south of Washington just outside Fredericksburg, Virginia. Civil War battlefields are to me as museums are to John. What a joy to be able to share!

We went first to the Chancellor House where the Union commander, General Joseph Hooker, called Fighting Joe by the press for his aggressive qualities, made his headquarters.

"It was a brilliant plan," I said in full guide mode. "Hooker's army was across the Rappahannock River from Fredericksburg, occupied by Lee's army. The way to Richmond went through Fredericksburg.

"Six months earlier the union army under General Burnside attacked Lee's army which had good defensive positions on the top of a ridge outside town, large parts of it protected by stone walls. The killing range of the musket then was well over five hundred yards. The result of men marching up a hill to attack men protected by stone walls with muskets lethal at long range was predictable: heaps and heaps of dead and wounded union soldiers, and defeat for Burnside. Among the wounded was future Supreme Court Justice, Oliver Wendell Holmes, a lieutenant in a Massachusetts regiment. He spent a cold, painful night lying wounded before that deadly wall.

"That was in December of the year. The following spring, Hooker, who had replaced Burnside, decided to have another go at Lee. This time, though, he would use stratagem rather than direct assault. He marched his army up the Rappahannock, crossed some twenty miles above Lee and put his army on Lee's flank. Grant would vainly try the same sort of thing over this same ground a year later. Now Lee had to attack him unless he wanted to leave Richmond vulnerable."

I swept my arm left and right. "Hooker's line was there, muskets loaded and waiting for Lee to come at them, reversing the situation at Fredericksburg months earlier. Hooker defending, Lee attacking."

I was pleased I had remembered so much. I glanced at John to see how he was taking it. He looked pensive. I pointed with my right arm to the hazy distance. "Out there was Hooker's right flank. It was unsecured."

"Unsecured?" John asked, giving me a funny look.

"Unprotected. To protect an open flank you bent the end of your line to make it perpendicular. Attackers would then face a prepared line of defense rather than the thin, naked end of your line. Jackson saw that (I looked at him to see if he knew who Jackson was, Lee's hell-devil second in command; he did) and made an end around march with his corps and hit Hooker hard. If it hadn't been late in the afternoon with darkness near, he might have rolled Hooker up, his battle not just lost but possibly his army destroyed as well."

"I gather that didn't happen," John said.

"No, darkness and the agile reaction of some of the Union officers out there, including a one armed general named Howard (after whom Howard University in DC was later named) saved the day, that and falling darkness. But Jackson was ready to finish the job at day break."

"Uh huh," John said, "and then what? " His interest was flattering. I knew when John was faking it, something we all learn in the diplomatic racquet. But I had his full attention. I swelled as I would have done if an ambassador had praised my just delivered report.

"Fortunately for Hooker, Jackson was shot that night by his own men as he was returning from a reconnaissance of the field for the next day's attack. The Confederate pickets mistook him and his staff for raiding Union cavalry. His arm was amputated that night and he died of pneumonia a week or so later"

"Ah, John exclaimed, "a deus ex machina. Lucky Hooker."

"He was," I said, really pleased by John's engagement.

"Overnight he reorganized his line and moved it back to those woods there," I said pointing at the country behind the Chancellorsville House. "He was in a strong defensive line, well positioned to inflect heavy damage on Lee should he attack. But Lee, decided first to deal with a threat against Fredericksburg by a corps Hooker had left there for the purpose. He detached a small force to watch Hooker and marched to meet the new challenge. Hooker took the opportunity to scoot back across the river and return meekly to his starting point."

"So much marching and so many casualties for that?" John dryly observed.

"You sound like some of Hooker's generals," I said. "The night before re-crossing the Rappahannock, Hooker held a war council. General Meade (later victor at Gettysburg) and several other generals argued strenuously against the move. They had a strong defensive position and wanted Lee to attack. But the fight had gone out of Hooker."

John shook his head. "I repeat, a lot for so little. Why even bother in the first place? War like a tennis match?"

"John," I said, "you've just defined the first three years of the war in the eastern theater. Every time the Union Army made a move in

Virginia, Lee gave them a hard knock and the Union Army retreated to rethink matters. Lee faltered only when he crossed the Potomac to attack. Antietam and Gettysburg were his rewards. . Grant changed all that."

"How so?"

"A year later when Grant becomes commander of all Union armies he made his headquarters with the Army of the Potomac, the one that fought here. He tried the same strategy Hooker tried-cross the river to get between Lee and Richmond and force him to attack, part of an overall strategy to wear Lee's army down by constant combat. Grant's superior forces could endure losses, Lee's couldn't.

"While Grant's army is marching through those woods (I point to our right front) Lee hits his flank, hard. It's another sharp blow. But this time instead of falling back to give matters another thought, as generals before him did, Grant orders his army forward. When his troops see this-fight, not flight-they let out a rolling whoop. Finally a general who knows how to fight to the finish. Union generals in Virginia had been like boxers retreating to their corner after a few blows. Grants gets in the ring with but a single thought; only one will leave this ring. The result, Appomattox."

As we walked back to our car John seemed lost in thought, his walking inattentive. Several times our hands accidentally touched. He gave me a half smile like a kid playing some secret, naughty little game. That day's sunshine remained with me for days.

CHAPTER TWENTY THREE

ALTERNATIVES ARE CONSIDERED

Thursdays were cabinet days. Jim Stevens had deliberately moved the cabinet meetings to a second floor room in Blair House with windows looking over Lafayette Park. The natural light of the room, the PM joked, would help bring transparency and clarity to cabinet decisions. The joke was only half serious. He often urged the cabinet to keep in mind the public that would be affected by what they did in that room. Glimpses of people walking about the park outside their windows helped.

Lafayette Square was a small page from the Republic's early history with the already remarked home of Secretary of State Seward along with, among others, St. John's Episcopal Church where many US presidents worshiped and the Decatur House, home of Stephen Decatur, naval hero of the War of 1812. The cabinet need only look out the window to be reminded of the river of history on which they were being carried.

There were three major items on the agenda.

The first concerned the National Health Care and Retirement Act of 202- which guaranteed every American full cradle to grave health care and a secure, comfortable retirement. The act was paid for by a combination of national VAT and dedicated taxes on certain Wall Street financial transactions.

The issue before the cabinet that morning was a proposed increase in the Wall Street tax to compensate for a modest jump in the cost of living.

Retirees received a monthly stipend based on an average of their life time annual earnings. There were three levels of graduation. Those with the lowest annual income level, up to $50,000.00, received the highest monthly stipend; those from $50,000.00 to $100,000.00 received the next lowest stipend; those from $100,000.00 and up received the smallest.

The steps were based on two broad assumptions: low income earners were in a poor position to put away much for retirement, little left after paying for food and housing. Those who earned a bit more could put something away for retirement but not to any significant degree. The highest earners could provide fully or in significant part for their own retirement.

The American worker should not have to depend on the vagaries of the market and corporate financial health and responsibility for the security of their retirement. Too many retirees had been screwed after promised company or state government pensions were reduced by inadequate funding or shrunken by bankruptcies or speculative corporate buyouts. American workers deserved better.

The usual protests arose on the House floor. "The Wall Street tax would destroy Wall Street as we know it and severely undermine the American way of life. Why should Wall Street be asked to support the retirement of America's workers, few of whom had ever worked for Wall Street?"

John Gilt, the Secretary of the Treasury, responded. "If less money stuffed in the pockets of its denizens by Wall Street meant one less Bentley in some broker's garage so that American workers enjoyed a secure, dignified retirement, so be it. After all, it was their labor in part that created the flow of wealth that makes Wall Street what it is. It's a fair exchange. Why should the public good have to depend on the voluntary generosity of the private sector? Everyone had to pay their fair share. If the common good is impoverished, eventually so will be the private sector. One can't be healthy without the other."

The cabinet approved the tax. The votes were there in the House to pass it.

The second item was looking for a new director of the National College of Defense Attorneys. By law, defense attorneys in criminal trials were to be drawn from the College at government expense. No more F. Lee Baileys,

The final item was the Russian question. Things were still on hold because of the Stapelton case.

"We can't keep temporizing without jeopardizing relations with the Kataev government. He is running his own risks by his opening to the West, and his opposition, quiet for the moment, is ready to exploit any sign suggesting bad faith on our part," the Prime said in leading off the discussion.

"We have to make a decision soon on the Smyrnov visit. There's no guarantee we'll ever know who put Novichok on Stapelton's lips and why. Meanwhile, Spurlock keeps poisoning the public well. We need an alternative. Any suggestions? "

Phil Brecken, Secretary of State spoke up. He was a modest sized man, unpretentious in appearance and mien but of extraordinary abilities. He was a representative from Massachusetts' North Shore, the country between Boston and Maine, a graduate of Stanford, and a Rhodes Scholar in history. "If I'm to be a coastal elite, at least let me be a bi coastal elite," he once said, explaining Stanford instead of the native Harvard. He had a common touch, which explained why Massachusetts kept returning him to the House, and an easy address when discussing complicated issues, his language clear, graceful and elevated without being grandiose or opaque.

"We don't really need Smyrnov to come here to advance the cause. His visit was meant to symbolize our opening to Russia and help consolidate public support. But Spurlock's attacks will make that less effective. Why not move the Smyrnov visit to Moscow? "

Most of the cabinet gave him puzzled looks. Only Jim understood Breckon's slightly off beat sense of humor.

"You mean you go there?"

"Exactly."

Jim laughed. "That will work. It will convince the Russians we still mean it and deny Spurlock an easy target."

"Except he'll just shift his fire to Phil," Robert Vance, Secretary of Defense, said. "True," Brecken answered, "but it won't offend the Russians the way attacks on Smyrnov would, and I'm used to his slings and arrows."

"Right. There'll still be press coverage, though it won't be quite the same," the Prime Minister said. "We'll just have to make the make the most of it." He looked up and down the cabinet table. "Are we agreed on Phil's suggestion?"

"It's a good idea, and I support it," Vance said, "but can we give the Smyrnov visit another week or so before we pull the plug? Having him come here is still the best idea, if we can neutralize Spurlock."

"Sounds reasonable," Stevens said. He checked the long, shiny table one more time. Universal nods. "OK, we are agreed. If the Stapelton issue stays as is, next week, Phil goes to Moscow."

Mike was not sure what to do. Everyone understood the problem: Spurlock. Until the suspicion of Russian involvement in Stapelton's death was eliminated, Spurlock still had a club.

He felt helpless. Unless someone voluntarily confessed-unlikely-he had no idea how they could effectively silence Spurlock before the week was out. The Smyrnov visit would be a bust, a poor advertisement for the prospects of the new relationship and a confusion to the public.

Reversing the old attitudes toward a hostile Russia would take time. Russia had been an adversary for too long, working to undermine US and Western interests. The few arms control measures demanded by mutual necessity were exceptions. Limited arms control treaties, yes;

universal disarmament for a stable world, no. That required a radical change in the climate.

To improve it and reset the political compasses of both nations would require more than an announcement by the Prime Minister. Concrete events leading in the new direction were needed. The Smyrnov visit was one such. Brecken's visit to Moscow, though of weaker immediate impact in the US, was another.

It was killing Mike he could do little to help neutralize Spurlock. He wished he could go straight for Spurlock's throat.

Ralph picked up on the third ring. "I know what you're going to ask me before you ask it," he said.

"You're a mind reader, too?" Mike said.

"With you? It's not so hard."

"OK, swami, so what's my question?"

"Any leads?"

"How'd you know?"

"Like I said, with you it aint hard. And the answer is, I'm still looking."

Mike knew it wasn't wise to reveal cabinet decisions before they had been made public. But by now he trusted Detective Barody-skip that-Ralph, implicitly.

"This is for your ears only, no one else. We have a week to find out who put Novichok on Stapelton's body. If not, the cabinet has decided on a slight change of direction."

"They want to scrap the whole thing?"

"Just a slight change, Ralph. Brecken will go to Moscow instead of having Smyrnov come here."

"Not the same impact, is it?" Ralph said.

Ralph's quick political instincts no longer surprised Mike. Ralph referred to himself as a dumb cop, but Mike knew that was camouflage. People thinking they were dealing with a dumb cop often made fatal mistakes. Actually, Ralph saw with the eye of an eagle and struck just as swiftly.

"No, it doesn't. But we can't wait forever for the best situation. The Russians might get antsy if this drags on. The Secretary of State in Moscow is better than nothing. We need to keep moving forward, even if it is more slowly than we'd like."

"Yeah, I can see that. Ok, mum's the word here. I like keeping secrets. It's what cops do. Anyway, to answer your basic question, no news, yet."

"Yet?"

"Patience, my friend. Cop work isn't like other things. You can't make a schedule for the way things will happen. There's a lot we don't control. All we can do is keep pushing until something breaks. Ninety percent of the time, something will, we just can't say when."

"OK, I appreciate that. I'm not trying to pressure you. It's just that I'm a little desperate. I can't tell you how it grinds me down to see a good man like Jim Stevens stymied by assholes like Spurlock. There's a history there. Spurlock is an angry bitter man, willing do anything to bring Jim Stevens down. It goes back to Kentucky when they were both up and coming politicians. I'll tell you about it someday.

"Something to look forward to. But for now, I'm pretty sure there's no Russian involvement, rogue or otherwise. We've checked the Russian arrivals in country going back a month before Stapelton's body was found. Nada, nobody who looks like an assassin. They wouldn't send anyone without diplomatic immunity. Way too dangerous. The embassy roster, same thing. No obvious candidates. If Russians are involved, they did a bang up job covering their tracks. My view, Russia is low on the list of suspects. Somebody here is my guess."

"Any real leads?"

"Maybe, but I'm not saying right now. Too early. One thing, though, this Stapelton didn't seem to have a lot of friends. Not surprising, I guess, since he spent most of his time working at overseas and all. But it does cut down the number of possible leads. Still, I got a few places to look. I'm working it. I'll get back to you when I have something.

"OK. Thanks. Talk later."

Working it? With so few leads? Mike wondered if he was looking at the Rasputin Circle. Seemed an unlikely place, but how many more leads were there? For a brief second he thought of calling Ralph back and reminding him of the Rasputins. But he had mentioned them already. To do it again would be insulting. Ralph knew his business. In any case, he would have found out about them on his own even if Mike had not mentioned them.

Was he right about the Russian embassy? During the Cold War and the Putin era almost anything could have been believed of a Russian embassy, a significant part of whose staff could have been KGB or FSB of one kind or another, a few of whom at least would be wet stuff attaches.

But now? The whole point of the Kataev/Stevens exercise was things were changing in fundamental ways. Russia no longer looked at itself as the natural enemy of other Nations, armed against them. It wanted to join the family of nations. Most families' didn't list murder among their neighborly activities. His relations with Elam were a strong suggestion of that.

CHAPTER TWENTY FOUR

NOTHING GETS EASIER

"Hope you aren't letting your anger get the better of you," she said. Louise knew how to read the signs.

What makes you say that? "

"Nothing specific. But I can always tell with you. When you're calm on the surface, you're often roiling below. Your calm is deceiving."

"You hanging out a shingle?"

"Thinking of it. You reveal a lot by the way you sleep."

"What, you're taking notes while I sleep?" He was only half annoyed.

"When you aren't agitated about something, you're as calm as a log. Sometimes I half wonder if you haven't checked out, you're so still. When your mind is troubled, you're a mini volcano, tossing and turning, muttering in your sleep. That's been you the last few days."

Mike's office was right next to the PM's with a nice view of Lafayette Park, General Jackson, horse rearing, hat held high, like a sword. Jackson wasn't Mike's idea of a model president. There was that business with the Cherokees, chasing perfectly peaceful and democratically functioning Indians out of the South so greedy whites could grab their land. There was also his history of dueling, occasionally with fatal bloodshed, though that was well before he was president. Jim Stevens would never have countenanced either act had he been a politician at the time. But Jackson did defend the Union against Calhoun and South Carolina, telling them if the state tried to secede over a dispute about tariffs, they'd painfully regret it. That stood in his favor. Jim Stevens would have done the same. So all in all, having the flinty old general stare straight into his small office wasn't a complete minus, as long as he kept thinking of South Carolina.

"Yeah, well I'm having a hard time keeping my perspective about Spurlock. The man has an unlimited capacity for making trouble. If it was just petty politics, I could handle it. But your Dad working to make important changes in our relations with Russia, ones that will affect the entire West in important ways, and all that asshole can do is carp. Not even any ideas of his own on how to respond to Kataev, just the same old bromides from the Cold War. To his rigid mind and shriveled soul all Russians are just Putin in different suits, the Russia of today no different from the Russia of Stalin, just more cars. With such crippled thinking he presumes to oppose a possibly earth shaking policy change because he doesn't like the policy maker? He wants to take your Dad down any way he can. Yeah, I'm pissed."

He studied Jackson. Why not send him galloping in Spurlock's direction? Jackson did know what to do with policy jerks. Just ask John Calhoun.

"He's a nasty man," Louise said with a sigh. "I've often wondered what about Dad makes Spurlock so angry and bitter. Political differences are one thing, but this is . . . .," her unfinished sentence trailed off in frustration.

"It goes back to Kentucky," Mike said.

"Yeah, I know it starts there. But just different sides of the aisle comes to this?"

Mike gave her a strange look.

"You mean you don't know?" he said, mildly stunned. How could she not know? She was already working closely with her father at the time. Had he deliberately kept this from her, protecting her?

"Your father never told you?"

"Told me what?"

"About Thom Davis's funereal and Spurlock's daughter?"

"Meredith? What does she have to do with it?"

Mike told her.

She stared at him, stunned. "This some kind of bad movie script?"

"I'm sure Spurlock wished it was," he said.

"All I remember is Spurlock resisted giving Mr. Davis a state funereal, and then he didn't. I just assumed he and Dad had talked."

Mike laughed. "Yeah, there was talk alright, but not by your Dad. It was me. I dealt with the snake."

"And he changed his mind because you talked to him about Meredith's abortion?"

Mike nodded. "The subject came up," he said tight lipped.

"Sounds to me like it more than came up. You threatened him?" she asked, a mixture of alarm and admiration.

"I pointed out certain realities he might have been overlooking in the matter of a funeral for Thom Davis," Mike said. He felt a little sheepish. It had all been so long ago.

She gave him a long look and then laughed. "My, my," she said with a put on Irish brogue, "Mike Sullivan, and him with his choir boy's face. I don't know whether to laugh or cry. Poor Meredith."

"She came out of it OK, and it was a long time ago," Mike said, wishing now to change the subject.

"Evidently not as far as Spurlock's concerned," she said with a slight rise in her voice.

Mike shrugged. "A sore loser. Most politicians would have moved on. It is the nation's loss that he hasn't".

"Maybe," she said doubtfully.

CHAPTER TWENTY FIVE

SOMEBODY WILL PAY

From the diary of Paul Fordney: THOSE SONS OF BITCHES!!! They have turned John down.

I cannot believe it! Turned him down!!! The best man by far for the job and turned down, casually, off handedly turned down, as if he was just asking for a day more to finish his report.

Oh, by the way John, your name won't be on the list of names for Moscow we're sending to the PM's office to replace David Noah.

JOHN STAPELTON is not good enough to replace that sleepy old place holder Noah!!!???

Give me a fucking break! John has forgotten more about Russia than Noah ever knew.

And he's not even on the list? Come fucking on!

I'd love to see the names that are on the list. Weak kneed, bureaucratic head nodders all, party line spouters, that's what they are. I don't need to see the names. People talking that sick old namby pamby peace party line, kiss the Russian and the Russian will kiss you back. Yeah, with a boot.

Nobody knows Russia the way John knows Russia, and nobody has the balls John has to deal with that slippery crowd in the Kremlin. He put it to Putin and he'd put it to that front man, Kataev, too, and all those KGBnicks manipulating him behind the scenes. John would see right through that little game and call it for what it is: a scheme to gull our peace loving, Kumbaya singing Prime Minister and set him up for a nice bait and switch. Yes, withdraw from NATO, drop your sanctions and give us full membership in the EU and peace will descend like a perfumed cloud over us all.

John saw right through that. He knows when the Kremlin is lying. Every time their lips move. John knew that better than anyone how to stick it to that moral dwarf, Putin. John had his number. With John in Spasso House firmly ensconced in the ambassadorial residence, he'd have Kataev's number, too.

If John had a fault, it was his truth telling when a little silence might have done him better. I tried to nudge him to be restrained when he was over at State schmoozing, lunch with an old friend or office hopping to lobby for the Moscow job. John, I'd say, you hurt yourself when you keep telling those geniuses at State how wrong they are. You know as well as I do that puts them off.

As I feared, it happened. John was having lunch with Lou Good, apparently trying to nudge his candidacy forward. I would have cautioned a little indirection, but John is nothing if not self-confident. He sometimes underrates the capacities of others, especially their intelligence and discernment. He assumes they rate his abilities as highly as he does. It leads him at times to wag a reckless tongue.

I don't know what he said to Lou, but obviously it had to do with who would be nominated by State to take Noah's place in Moscow. He will retire before next summer. Good told John, and I expect with some malicious glee, he wasn't at liberty to say who was on the list or whose name the department was putting forward to replace Noah, but in fairness to John he could say it would not be his.

In all reason, John, given your views on Russian/American relations, how could you possibly expect the Secretary of State to make you the government's representative in Moscow? Your views, which you do nothing to hide, and which you spread across the editorial pages of the Post with great abandon, are a hundred eighty degrees opposed to the government s.

So that's it. Truth must give way to politics.

John is too good for such a world.

When John told me, he hid his disappointment like the classy guy he is. He takes his lumps gracefully. Puts to shame those whiners at Foggy Bottom.

They will pay!!

CHAPTER TWENTY SIX

THE RASPUTINS GROW NERVOUS

Have any of you been contacted by a Detective Barody from the Metropolitan Police? Jim Pernick asked.

The Rasputins were meeting at one of their faux British pubs on Capitol Hill, ironically chosen months earlier because it was near John Stapelton's Capitol Hill townhouse.

Every hand went up.

"I was afraid of that," Pernik said.

"What's going on?" Fred O Brien asked.

"What did they ask you?" Pernick asked.

"Just a lot of stuff about John," O Brien replied. "Who were his friends, did he have any enemies who might want to do him harm, you know, things like that."

"How about you," Pernick asked Schulick.

"Yeah, about the same."

"And nothing about Russians being involved?" Pernick asked.

Both men shook their heads.

"So?" O Brien said. "Should he?"

"Not if he doesn't think Russians are involved. His questions suggest he might think otherwise, an American, in fact."

"An American!" O Brien exclaimed. "You think he suspects one of us?"

"If you were a cop, wouldn't you check out his friends and acquaintances? Most murder victims are known to their murderer. Of course we're suspects. But that's not what bothers me."

"So what does bother you?" Schulick asked.

"If this Detective Barody is focusing on local suspects, it means Russian involvement is ruled out. And Governor Shaw? Has he changed his mind, too? That would leave us exposed."

"How?" O'Brien asked.

"Our thesis is no longer taken seriously."

"Our thesis?" O Brien asked, stupidly, Pernick thought.

"That John was killed by FSB rogue elements."

"Oh, right, that," O'Brien said hastily.

Pernick suppressed the sarcastic retort he felt coming on. O Brien had good contacts among theater people in Washington, helpful when good tickets were hard to find.

"So what do you propose?" Paul Fordney asked, silent up until now. There were times when he and Pernick acted on the assumption they were the only two adults in the room, especially when political issues were under discussion.

"Remind the world, or at least this small part of it, that the real culprit is to be found in Russia, not Washington."

"I sense an editorial coming on," Fordney said smugly.

"You do indeed," Pernick said.

A few days later an editorial under Jim Pernick's name duly appeared in the Washington Post.

The headline read "Are the Police Taking Their Eye off the Ball in the Stapelton Case?"

"There is absolutely no evidence," the piece went on, "that John Stapelton was killed by anyone other than an operative of the Russian state. No one in the United States has access to Novichok. Even if they did, would they use it in such a garden variety street mugging? Only Russia has Novichok and only Russia has ever used it on a human being. Our thesis is, rogue elements of the Russian FSB, still loyal to the memory of that late, unlamented thug, Vladimir Putin, used Novichok to kill American Foreign Service Officer John Stapelton. They had both motive and means. John Stapelton was a diplomatic thorn in the side of the tin pot Russian dictator, and FSB operatives have used Novichok before, most notably in an attempt to silence Russian intelligence defector Sergei Skripel and his daughter several years ago in Great Britain.

"Enough said?"

CHAPTER TWENTY SEVEN

A LEAD

This the Prime Minister's special assistant?" The voice was muffled.
"Who's this?"

"Who is not important. I have information about the Stapelton case."

Mike paused, suspicious but intrigued.

"Yes? Go ahead."

"Ask Paul Fordney how he knows Zviad Tabidze at Fort Detrick."

"Who *is* this?" Mike repeated. There was a click and then silence.

He sat there for a moment, not knowing what to think. A crank call? Not likely. Paul Fordney and Zviad Tabidze were not names in the news, there to be the play things of any wandering crack pot. The caller had some kind of insider information. Why had he called? What should Mike do about it?

The question was too important to ignore, suspect though its generation was.

He tapped in Ralph's number.

"I just got an anonymous call, said I should ask Paul Fordney how he knows Zviad Tabidze."

Ralph paused. "Could be a lead. Anonymous, you say?"

"Right."

"Maybe a crank call, or somebody looking to hurt Fordney. Still,

Its gotta be checked out. It could be the break we're looking for, and there's little risk."

"What I thought. Can I ask a favor?"

"This early in the morning?" Ralph asked. "Sure, go ahead."

"I assume you will want talk to him. Can I get to him first?"

More silence. Then, "Yeah, OK. It's not a murder case. If he's the guy who left the body with Novichok, those are felonies, but they're far down the scale. Murder, might be a different matter. Risk of flight, for one thing. But this is OK. Go ahead, talk to him first, then let me know."

"Will do. Thanks."

He told the PM. "I'm going to talk to him, see what this is about. On the face of it, this could really be big."

"This Tabidze is who?"

"Former Soviet Georgian national working at Fort Detrick in Frederick, Maryland. He's in charge of nerve agents, including Novichok."

The Prime Minister gave a low whistle "What a lot of coincidences. Yeah, you have to check it out. I assume you've told the police?"

"I have. He said I could have first crack."

OK, keep me informed. We have a week before we need to make up our minds about Brecken's visit. Would be nice to settle this before."

"Got it. For the first time, I'm excited. Might be something here."

"Fingers crossed," the PM said, holding up his right hand to show his fingers were in the right place.

Fordney answered on the third ring.

Mike identified himself. "I understand you are an acquaintance of John Stapelton's?"

"I am. We served in Moscow together. We were also members of a group of former Foreign Service officers stationed in Moscow. Wet meet once a month."

"Yes, I know. The Rasputin Circle. I've already talked to Jim Pernick."

"Yes, he told me. So how can I help you, Mr. Sullivan?"

"Are you free for lunch, next day or two, possibly?"

"Can't we do this over the phone?"

"Is your phone secure?"

There was a hesitation. "This is classified?"

"It could involve sensitive matters."

"I see. You need a secure facility?"

"No need to go that far. Any discrete setting will do where privacy is assured. Perhaps you can suggest something that would fit the bill?"

"There's a Russian restaurant out here in McLean. It's called The Boyar. They serve great Pereskia, the Russian version of pierogi. Like to try that?"

"Sounds great. Tomorrow OK?"

"I'm retired. My time's my own. Noon? I'll text you the address and directions."

"That's very kind. See you tomorrow at noon."

After he hung up, Paul Fordney wondered, could he possibly know something about John and me? He was career CIA. He knew how the government can find stuff out.

Mike drove an unmarked car from the government motor pool. The attractive neighborhoods of McLean were in full leaf, some just beginning to turn. McLean, not too far from Langley, was chosen by many C IA officers as their place or retirement. Other parts of the extensive Northern Virginia suburbs were likewise populated by US government officials, both working and retired, most liberal in politics to the extent these suburbs were referred to sarcastically as North Vietnam by Richmond's conservative assemblymen.

Fordney's directions guided him to a small shopping center of posh shops of red brick and faux Victorian store fronts. The parking lot was filled with tall, old oaks which cosseted with dignified shade the many parked Mercedes, BMWs, Lexus and other bragging rights cars.

The Boyar was not hard to find. It was at the far end of the line of shops. The sign gilding the brick wall above a Victorian bay window said in gold imitation Cyrillic characters on a red field "The Boyar." It had to be the restaurant.

Mike looked for a middle aged man sitting by himself, away from other diners. It was a Tuesday and the restaurant was not crowded. Mike found his man easily, sitting in a back corner.

"Mike Sullivan," he said holding out his hand which Fordney took.

"Fordney," he said. "You're easy to spot from your picture in the papers and on TV."

Mike nodded.

"Let me recommend the Pereskia with a side. Have you had them before?"

"No, this is a first", Mike said. "Russian dumplings, I'm told?"

"Yes. Parenthetically, they were a favorite of John Stapelton's in Moscow. He loved stopping in these little enclosed stands that served nothing but Pereskia, a popular street food. The windows are all steamed up in winter, making for a warm, cozy atmosphere. Customers sit on bar stools at these high, round tables. There's nothing quite like them here in the US".

Mike looked around.

"No, they don't do that here. It's a full restaurant. The menu is very good, all Russian. The Pereskia are special. They come filled with cheese, potato or ground meat and are fried or boiled. Toppings are vinegar, sour cream or fried onions."

Mike ordered his meat filled, fried and with vinegar. He had a side of Borscht.

After the food had come and they had tucked in, Fordney said, "I'm curious about your interest in John Stapelton. Surely it's a police matter? The PM 's office must have more important things to do?"

"True enough if it weren't entangled in our Russian policy. Unfortunately . . ." he said, letting the rest of the sentence trail off.

"It is entangled."

"Something you surely know. The Washington Post's editorial pages are loud with the Rasputin Circle's eloquent criticisms of the Prime Minister's Russian policy. I can do no better than cite the most recent piece by Mr. Pernick in yesterday's edition. 'Rogue FSB, no other possible answer."

"Well, one can understand why you might think otherwise. Rather inconvenient to your policy, is it not? Perhaps Congressman Spurlock has put it best. Why are we making friends with those who murder American citizens on American soil? But I'm sure you didn't come here to debate the point. You said you wanted to ask about John Stapelton?"

"Actually, I do have another question in mind. But before getting to that, I'm curious about one thing."

"Which is?" Fordney asked, a bit wary.

"I assume you know Stapelton died of a heart attack. It wasn't Novichok."

"I am. But I don't see that changes anything. No one outside Russia uses Novichok. I'm not sure what the link is between John's heart attack and the Novichok except that it was present on his body. Nobody but Russia uses that stuff. Rogue FSBs make as much sense as anything else. They want to embarrass the US and Kataev because they oppose this detente. It diminishes the importance of uncovering traitors and catching spies. Actually, not a bad idea dropping the FSB a peg or two, though I'm sure that's not what either Kataev or Stevens have in mind.

"The thesis of rogues at least offers a reasonable explanation for the known facts. I don't need to recite them again for your benefit. You know them as well as I do. Probably better. You dispute their meaning for obvious reasons, it undercuts your Russian policy. But my thesis explains things better than yours. So it was a heart attack," he said, shrugging. "To me, all that means is what was meant to be a murder weapon just became a calling card. Really changes nothing."

There was some merit to the argument. The known facts could be read that way. This Fordney knew his brief, Mike thought, and until solid counter facts were available the thesis had life.

"One can make that case, I'll admit. But, it won't stop either Kataev or Stevens from moving ahead, if more slowly. Difficulties are there to be overcome. They delay, but they don't deter."

"A nice speech. I can see why you do what you do. You serve your boss well. I agree, John's death, even if by FSB rogues, won't derail the Stevens/Kataev rapprochement. But it does raise the question, how much can Russia really be trusted? You believe the bear can be made a house pet, we, who know a thing or two about Russia, don t. The bear's not for taming. Do we need say more?"

"Probably not. I disagree with your arguments, but I understand the logic. But as I said, I didn't come out here to debate that issue with you. It' another matter that concerns me."

"And what might that be," Fordney said with an obvious show of patience."

"I'm told you have a relationship with a certain Zviad Tabidze. That raises a concern that needs to be cleared up. You can guess why I might be asking."

Fordney stared hard at him, really hard. "How did you get that name?" he finally asked as coldly as he could.

"It has been provided to the PM's office."

Mike felt a little silly saying that. "Anonymous" was treacherous ground. Without an actual human face behind it, information had to be suspect in the extreme. Fordney, for all his aberrant political views, was no fool. If Mike had said "anonymous caller," Fordney would have laughed in his face. Even so, Mike had to pursue the lead, as Ralph would have. That was good enough for Mike.

Fordney looked off to the side, thinking.

Looking back at Mike, he said I'm assuming you know who I worked for and that I spent two tours in Moscow?"

Mike nodded. "At the embassy, yes".

"At the embassy but not entirely *of* the embassy."

"I get your point. We don't have to pussy foot. I know your work was of a highly sensitive nature, not the kind of thing to be openly discussed."

"To say the least. I am free to talk about almost noting of what I did while serving in Moscow."

"But you do know a certain Zviad Tabidze who also lived in Moscow at one time?"

"I can't answer that, and that's all I can say on the subject. We are in highly classified territory here, and I am not at liberty to discuss any of it with any one. There is an agreement forbidding it, signed by me. If the

PM wants to know more, he will have to address himself to the Director at Langley. But I warn you, there are some things the Agency does not discuss outside its four walls, not even with the Prime Minister. Now, if you will excuse me, this conversation is over."

With that he got up, took some money from his wallet, dropped it on the table saying, "This should cover my share," and left.

Mike felt jilted. He sat there for several minutes to collect his thoughts and give Fordney a chance to clear the shopping center. Meeting accidentally outside would be mutually embarrassing. Then he fished some money from his wallet, dropped it on top of Fordney's and left as well.

On his way back down the George Washington Parkway, intermittent views of the rock strewn Potomac flashing by, he tried to pin down what it was about this Fordney that made him look like a typical member of the security state's upper reaches but also different. He had the same thoughtful intellectual air mixed with that look of the bureaucratic activists who used to acting and knowing why and what they acting about, people well beyond the highly paid pencil pushers level."

Fordney had that look but also something different. It was that something different Mike couldn't find words for.

The man was moderately tall, six one, perhaps, and free of excess weight and even though in his late fifties or early sixties had no after youth softness or signs of a middle age spread. His neatly trimmed mustache gave a slightly British cast to his lean somewhat ascetic face, the face of a man who may have seen his share of life but was marked by it in ways different from other men. It was the face of a man who was born middle aged, free of the scars that get most men there.

He was a bachelor-Mike had done some basic research before heading out to McLean-and perhaps that was it. The marks left by the cares of marriage and child rearing on others were absent from this man's face.

From the pages of Paul Fordney's diary. **Who the fuck is talking??** Sullivan did not get that name from thin air.

It can't be anyone from the Agency. The culture and its prohibitions are too strong. Not even in the throes of the most violent bureaucratic infighting would someone do that, reveal the name of an opponent's asset. *That just isn't done.*

Who else would know anything about Zviad, as he now calls himself? His name was changed after we got him out of Russia, part of his new identity. At first I thought a Georgian name a bad choice. Lots of Soviets have Georgian names. But the cover story was brilliant.

Which goes: Zviad is the son of Konstantin Tabidze, a Soviet Georgian soldier captured by the Germans in the Ukraine in 1943. He was turned by the Germans and served in Vlahos's corps of Soviet POWs now fighting for the Germans. Konstantin was captured by us in Normandy and turned over to the French. The French gave him a choice: repatriation to the Soviet Union (certain death) or eight years in the French Foreign Legion fighting in Viet Nam against the Viet Min insurgency (a considerably less certain death) After fulfilling his obligations to the French, Konstantin landed in Brazil from which he eventually emigrated to the US. Zviad was born in Brazil, hence his accent. Konstantin became a broadcaster in the VOA's Georgian Service having been issued a special visa by the USG for the purpose.

Do I know Zviad Tabidze? I won't answer that, not even on these pages. I shouldn't be writing even this much, but I know enough about encryption to keep this from anyone's eyes but the Agency's, and it already knows all this.

Do I know Zviad Tabidze? Not really. I've deliberately kept my distance largely because the Agency said I should. And I'm not comfortable with a man who betrayed his country, even if it was for our benefit.

But did I know the man who became this Zviad Tabidze?

Did I?

So well I could write a best seller about our relationship. How we got him out of Russia when the walls were closing in would make a full chapter all by itself. Part of a group of Russian tourists going to Helsinki for a long weekend; surreptitiously slipping away from the group and taking an overnight ferry to Stockholm where he was met by our people and given a whole new set of documents-passport, Maryland driver's license, US social security card, the works, including the deed to a house in Myersville, MD, in his new name, and a job at Fort Detrick with picture ID card, all this before he steps foot on the SAS flight that takes him to New York. That he was a bachelor and this now the Russian Federated Republic rather than the USSR made it all easier.

Did I know him? Perhaps more than I wanted to.

But my question is, who the fuck gave up this name? Not anyone in the Agency. First of all, there aren't that many who know about him. Everything was closely kept in the Russian division, and nobody but nobody there talks.

But it has to be somebody with Moscow experience. Somehow somebody in the embassy must have stumbled on the secret.

I recall an incident that might explain how.

The Press Attaché invited a number of his Russian media contacts for cocktails. One of them, a journalist from Novi Mir, a Russian literary magazine famous for publishing Alexander Solzhenitsyn's One Day in the Life of Ivan Denisovich, lingered after the other guests had departed.

The host thought this a little odd, there being no special relationship between the two, but still freshened his guests drink. The man said he wanted to talk about the writings of one Pavel Mularchick.

His host didn't recognize the name. "Pavel Mularchick," the Russian repeated.

His host remained lost. "Who?"

The Russian looked stricken. He asked if he could use the bathroom. His host told him where it was and waited. When the journalist reappeared, he said he noticed his host had a copy of Hemingway's For Whom the Bells Toll in his library. "I've always thought Chapter Four particularly interesting," the Russian said. With that he left.

By this time Herb Taylor-not his real name-had his suspicions. His guest might be a CIA asset, the name Pavel Mularchick some kind of recognition signal.

Herb went to the copy of For Whom the Bells, opened to Chapter Four, and sure enough there was a slip of paper with something incomprehensible written on it and in clear English the name of an officer in our section. Clearly a drop of some kind.

Herb took it to our people on the eighth floor. They immediately knew what it was and warned Herb not to mention it to anyone. Herb said, "right, but next time make sure you give him the name of a real spook." The sarcasm was justified.

I tell this to show that Neizvestny (FBI note. Neizvestny is Russian for unknown) might have made a similar error, revealing his identity to some innocent by mistake.

But who?

Only one name is possible. Somehow that self-important, name dropping, wheeze bag Pernick knows about Tabidze and Fort Detrick and notified the PM's office. He suspects something about John and me and is jealous. He cannot bear it that John, one of State's leading Russian policy analysts, chose me as a friend rather than him, Mr. Russian Policy himself.

Well, if I have anything to say about it, he has dropped his last name.

CHAPTER TWENTY EIGHT

SOME LOOSE THREADS START TO COME TOGETHER

Mister Speaker,"I ask the Prime Minister to clarify for this house the purpose of the proposed visit of Secretary of State Brecken to Moscow. Is it to avoid further embarrassment over the affair Stapelton? If so, the Prime Minister is certainly wise to postpone the visit by Foreign Minister Smyrnov whose presence in this fair city would do nothing but throw a more intense light on the unresolved issues raised by the death of retired American Foreign Service Officer, John Stapelton. How can it be this government is willing to welcome to these shores the representative of a government which has either directly by the action of one of its own agents or indirectly by the action of rogue elements in its security apparatus committed an affront against this great nation. In either case how can one trust a government which is either nefariously hypocritical or dangerously ineffective in controlling the members in its own ranks who murder an innocent American in our very midst? I ask this house how it can accept the indignity of this government welcoming in our nation's capital a high representative of such a government?"

Prime Minister Stevens got up to respond.

"Mister Speaker, as usual the remarks by the honorable gentleman from Kentucky far exceed in hyperbole what they lack in logic or fact.

And yes, if Secretary of State Brecken goes to Moscow, it will be to further the work he and Foreign Minister Smyrnov have so effectively begun. This government will not let mysteries or ill-founded doubts deter it from the important work of making the world a more secure and peaceful place for all its people. If this government thought for one moment that President Kataev was pursuing better relations with one hand while committing murder in our own back yard with the other, I would suspend negotiations immediately and demand an immediate explanation. I do not believe that is the case and will not let minor interruptions deflect us from our course.

"Only Russia has Novichok? No, we have it too, though securely under lock and key at Fort Detrick. Others may have it as well.

"Is the honorable member for Kentucky that sure of his grounds? Can he assure this house there is no terrorist organization that has secured Novichok and has used it to embarrass both us and the Russians?

"This house would be greatly relieved if the honorable gentleman could do so, or barring that, prove that president Kataev has blatantly lied to me, or that rogue Russian elements are not behind the lamentable death of an American citizen?

"In the meantime, the government will continue to pursue our determined course despite the ill-founded and partisan hesitations of the opposition. The responsibility is ours and we joyfully shoulder it.

"Is the opposition ready to do the same?"

Who was it said it is darkest just before the dawn? Mike would have occasion to remember that old piece of folk wisdom. But first he and Ralph were meeting at McDonald's again.

"It aint high cuisine, but it tastes good," Ralph observed. They were meeting almost once a week now. Mike needed to feel he was doing all he could to solve the Stapelton mystery, and Ralph did so because he was sensitive to Mike's need.

"News?" Mike asked, unwrapping his Big Mac.

"Maybe," Ralph replied after a first bite.

"Maybe?" Mike said.

"Friend of mine on the Maryland State Troopers, Frederick Barracks, left a message, said he might have something. He was out on a case when I called back. So I'm waiting. He must have something, just don't know what. I'll let you know."

They were only three bites into their meals.

So, not much more to be said on that front, I guess," Mike said. "But there is something else I'd like to ask you about. Totally unrelated to Stapelton."

"Shoot," Ralph said.

"I assume you're familiar with the government's proposal to form a criminal defense attorney's bureau to handle the defense in all criminal cases. No more private defense attorneys. Do the police have an opinion?"

"Well, I'm no pundit and I can't speak for the police, but I can imagine how the rich will howl. No more calling F Lee Bailey when trouble strikes? On the other hand, people from the hood will like it just fine. Middle class, too, probably. Personally I'm fine with it. Don't know how other cops feel, if that's what you're asking. Still, too new."

"You're OK with it? Don't think it's socialism or a government takeover?"

"What if it was? Question is, will it work? Will lawyers work as hard for the government as they would for themselves?"

"Lawyers who work for the Justice Department seem to. Like career military, dedication to the profession and a desire to succeed is for them the incentive money is for others. Of course they're well paid, too. Just that nobody gets rich."

"You got a point there. Can't say any of these private security cops are better than real cops. Worse, in most case. So yeah, I guess you'd get a good lawyer if one was assigned to you. That's how it works? You get charged, the government assigns you a lawyer from this, what is it, college?"

"Yeah, college."

"Why college? I thought Harvard was a college? I gather this aint Harvard. "

"No, it aint. College. Basic meaning of the word is a group of people performing a common function with defined rights and privileges. "

Ralph laughed. "Okay, glad to know. Can you choose a lawyer? I'm mean there's going to be good ones and not so good ones."

"You can ask, but in the end you'll have to take what is offered. You can't choose your own lawyer any more than you can choose your own judge or jury. Military does it that way all the time. They'll all have to meet a certain standard, just as lawyers at Justice do. Some guy who took five tries before passing the bar won't make the cut. They will all have to show they can handle any kind of criminal case."

"So how about expenses, like hiring expert witnesses, gathering evidence, stuff like that. Who pays that?"

"The college, the government."

"Really! Boy that levels the playing field. Cops are not lawyers, but we know a fair amount about how trials go, testifying and all the way we have to. I've seen the difference an expensive expert can make in a trial. The O J trial proves that. Experts? Hell, expensive lawyers, too. Big difference sometimes. Got O J off. Most guys from the hood couldn't touch that kind of defense. Most middle class guys, too, for that matter. Not without mortgaging the house. So the point is, money should not determine the kind of defense you get?"

"In a nut shell."

Ralph finished his sandwich and slurped the last of his drink. "Well, I can see the point of it all. Count me aboard."

"I was betting with myself you would be," Mike said.

"But just out of curiosity, what brought all this on?" Spurlock and them will just holler more socialism."

"Let them. The Prime Minister welcomes the title."

"Guy's got balls," Ralph said admiringly.

"Justice is not a private good," Mike continued, "like a car or a house, quality determined by your wallet. It's a basic function of any well-ordered society, and as such its quality and fairness should not have to depend on the size of your bank account."

"Yeah, I like that," Ralph said. "For one thing, it will makes us feel better when we run in some guy with nothing but a hoodie and a pair of sneakers to his name. With this we know he'll get a real defense, not whatever crappy deal his court appointed lawyer cuts before moving onto the next case."

"OK," Mike said. "I'm glad you're down with it. That's good to hear. Now I can report to the PM that a finely tested poll shows the middle class supports a college of criminal defense lawyers."

Ralph laughed. "Right, the people have spoken. OK, gotta goes. Some of us work, you know, "he said, giving Mike his least sincere smile.

"Go," Mike said. "Let me know what you hear from the Frederick Barracks."

"Will do."

CHAPTER TWENTY NINE

NIGHT OF ECSTASY. NIGHT OF HORROR

From the diary of Paul Fordney: I can barely write this, my hand is shaking so. But I must, for the sake of the record. For 'sake. Is it possible to have the happiest, most glorious night of your life and the most horrifying? Tell me it is impossible, that all this is a bad dream, a nightmare inflicted on me by my worst enemy. How have I managed to get this far without collapsing?

John and I went to this trendy little trattoria on Capitol Hill for an Italian meal. I spent a tour in Rome as a young officer and know what good Italian cooking is-delicate, balanced, subtly flavored, restrained, modest portions, Aristotelean, not Bacchanalian.

Most American Italian restaurants are far from that-gigantic portions, by Italian standards, meat cooked to a doneness rather peak flavor, and taste oversell in everything, the cuisine revolving around the garlic. In Italy, it's there, not revealing itself except in the way it enhances other flavors.

And pasta! Pasta is never the main course in any restaurant in Italy. It is the prelude to the main course of meat and vegetables; it is never served as a great heap covering the dinner plate, only enough for modest satisfaction, there to lead you onto the next course.

As for sauces! Every restaurant worthy of the name has its own special sauce.

My favorite was a sauce made by this restaurant outside Spoleto on a hillside amid olive groves overlooking the city. It made a pasta sauce from black truffles that was a perfect marriage of earthy and piquant.

I amused John with my toned down tirade. He actually knew what I was talking about. He has spent vacations in Italy, most enjoying southern Italy, Basilicata and Sicily, a taste I don't share. My enjoyment of Italy starts in Rome and goes north. If there is a *real* Italy, it is found somewhere in Umbria.

I'm rambling on about Italy to distract from the searing pain shriveling my soul. I shall never be able to share thoughts like these with John again. My life is over.

We finished the meal with a glass of grappa, the Italian answer to schnapps. As it was meant to, it settled our meal (this trattoria, whose name if Grappolo D Oro, comes as close to the Italian mean as anything I know in the US. John agreed) and sent a warmth through us loosening our tongues, or as loose as a diplomat's tongue ever get. We reminisced about good times we enjoyed together and said how fortunate we were to have each other. Most of our colleagues-men with whom we might be close friends-are married, making easy and frequent male socializing difficult since the spouse is a part of most socializing. No spouse, less socializing with marrieds. Things like golfing, which I don't do, or the Rasputin Circles are just a few of the times when you can socialize man to man. But things like that are hardly the venue for growing a really satisfying, intimate relationship.

I noticed John was dropping little endearments more than usual. He's restrained by nature, a State Department guy for sure. Yet tonight I was his heart's companion or the man who has enriched his life beyond measure, sweet words that had me glowing inside from more than the grappa.

As we got to the end of our grappa, John leaned back and said, "What a perfect evening. Why don't you come back to my place? I have some Napoleon brandy that is to die for."

As soon as we cleared the small entry hallway and were standing face to face in the living room John came close, took my face in both hands and said, "I hope you know how I feel about you," and before I could say anything, kissed me full on the lips. I don't know whose tongue engaged first, didn't even know if men could kiss that way, but suddenly both our tongues were involved in a mad tarantella with us stroking each other, whispering things to one another, things neither mouth would ever have formed without the stimulation of our bodies being locked together as though we were physically joined by nature.

Suddenly, John drew back, said, "How I have waited for this," took me by the hand as though a child and led me upstairs to his bedroom.

In a blur all my clothes were off, his hands an unveiling wind. I must have done the same to him because in the next instant we were together on his bed, naked, groaning and stroking, fondling and gasping and finally making love. I don't think either of us spoke, unless sighs and groans of pleasure are speech. We made love time and time again making up for lost time, each release like a powerful jet of water shooting up and falling back in a great shower.

Finally, we lay face to face, grinning at one another, laughing happily like two kids on a lark, stroking one another.

I was deliriously happy, deeply content, my joy gushing up like a new found spring. I was almost giddy and was about to crack wise-"John, you said something about brandy?"-when he began covering my face again with kisses and coming to one more mighty arousal. He slid over me and limned me like the bowl of a spoon, embracing me and putting his lips close to my ear. He entered me, turning my insides into warm pudding. I clamped my hands over his hand that was gently pressing on my aroused cock. His breathing was deep and passionate, his smooth, vigorous thrusts telling me how much he wanted me.

Suddenly there was a sharp gasp and John stiffened. I thought he had just had the mother all orgasms. I smiled to share his joy.

But something was wrong. I sensed it and then suddenly I felt alone.

At the moment of my, no, our greatest happiness, John had gone. Left. Departed after giving me the gift of himself.

I sat on the edge of the bed, stunned, feelings of soaring happiness mixed with piercing sadness. In the same blur of pleasure John and I had become one, and then John had gone, left this earth, I the last to be with him.

I don't believe in God, but if I did, I would know he had made this moment for a reason. But it wasn't God; it was destiny, the destiny of our two separate natures, one that led me into the CIA, the other leading John into the State Department where he became, in my opinion, State's leading expert on Russian affairs. Those two destinies had taken us to Moscow where we recognized each other as the incomplete half of the other and brought us finally to this bed in John's house on Capitol Hill in Washington, D.C. in the year 202-. This moment was the final chord of the symphony of our lives.

I sat there, asking myself, who had John been apart from my other half? He had been our most penetrating thinker on Russia and had worked tirelessly to keep our nation from fatally embracing its mortal enemy. The Lilliputians at State and Blair House had foiled him in this first iteration of his life, but they would not foil him in this, the second, the cadenced iteration of that life.

John had one more blow to strike and I had one more task to perform to help him strike it. I saw clearly the task before me, all that needed to be done. It was going to be a busy night, consuming most of the remaining darkness.

CHAPTER THIRTY

THE CIRCLE CLOSES

Mike went right to his phone the moment caller ID showed who it was.

"Yes Ralph."

"We might have something. "

"Finally," Mike breathed to himself.

"My friend called from the Frederick Barracks. Said he was looking over his records and something jumped out."

"Yeah?" Mike said, crossing and uncrossing his fingers, feeling a little stupid doing it-what did his fingers have to do with what that state trooper in Frederick might know-but so excited he had to do something.

"Ok, listen to this," Ralph said, understanding the effect his words, maybe drawing it out a little just to increase the dramatic tension. "On the night before Stapelton's body was found, he pulled somebody over for speeding. The person was heading for DC on 470, just by the Urbana Exit. It was eleven o clock at night."

Jesus, Ralph, the name, the name, Mike thought silently, biting his tongue, understanding Ralph was playing him, swearing he'd get even, but later, not now.

"Yeah?" he said.

"One of your friends from that Rasputin Circle."

As soon as Ralph said the name it all fit.

"Jesus," Mike said, "we should have guessed it."

"Well, we're not there yet, but we're close. We're going to pick him up for questioning."

"When?"

"Within the hour."

"Can I talk to him first? A favor?"

"Normally, the answer would be no. But you asking as a member of the Prime Minister's staff? It's official business?"

"Yes, of course."

"OK. I'm assuming you have good reason. In any case, if he runs, he won't get far. Go ahead, but don't tell him we are on the way to pick him up."

"OK. Thanks. I won't. That bastard owes us something, the trouble he's caused."

"OK. Good luck."

As soon as he clicked off, Mike dialed Paul Fordney's number. He answered on the ring as though he was holding the phone in his hand, waiting for the call.

"I'd ask to what do I owe the pleasure, Mr. Sullivan, but I'd be lying if I gave the impression I view this call as a pleasure."

"Yes, I imagine you don't. I can't believe you didn't know this call would finally come."

"Perhaps you imagine too much."

"Well, let's see. I'm going to cite a few facts and connect some dots. Let's start with this one. You were stopped for speeding on 470 out near Frederick the night before John Stapelton's body was discovered. You told the state trooper you had been visiting a friend in Frederick and were rushing home to let your dog out. He had been cooped up all day. The Maryland State Police barracks in Frederick verifies this.

"A few more dots. The friend you were visiting is, in fact, Zviad Tabidze. You wanted Novichok to put on Stapelton's body. Then you deposited your dead friend by Hamilton's statue. A nice touch, that. Perhaps you can explain what it means. Why Hamilton? Some special reason?

"But let that go for the moment. I want to connect a few more dots. Your intent was to accuse the Russians of John Stapelton's murder to discredit Russia and undermine the government's policy.

"How's this so far?"

"You have a rich imagination, Mr. Sullivan. You're in the wrong line of work. Fantasy mystery writer seems to suit you better."

"Time will tell whether I'm good at writing mysteries or you're better at concocting them. The Metropolitan Police have the same facts and connected the dots I do. I can't imagine they won't want to talk to you. There are two charges outstanding, improper disposal of a corpse and dangerous handling of a highly toxic material. Both are felonies and lead to some jail time. Jibe with me if you want. It won't be so easy with the police."

"How much longer do you propose continuing this charade, Mr. Sullivan? I'm on the verge of hanging up."

"I wouldn't do that, If I were you," Mike said, his voice suddenly hard. "I have a proposition to make."

"If it's as fanciful as your assumed facts and dots, I doubt I'd be interested."

"You judge. If you hang up now, you face the police and the prosecutor all on your own. You hear me out and cooperate, the PM's office might consider intervening to ask the prosecutor for leniency, possibly no jail time. Still want to hang up?"

"You're starting to make some sense. What do I have to do, stand in front of Blair House and recite the pledge of allegiance and promise to vote Americrat the rest of my life?"

"I'll let your weak attempt at humor pass. We aren't Republicans, 'You commit the crime, you do the time.' Something a bit more condign. You make a public statement in writing saying what you did and why you did it, express regret for the public inconvenience you caused, state your act was to embarrass the government and pin the blame on Russia. You deemed this your duty as an informed citizen. You now realize your emotional state at the death of your friend clouded your judgement and led you into an act you would not have made in a more equitable frame of mind. To show your good faith and make amends to the public, you will offer to perform some public service to be determined by the Attorney General of the Sate of Columbia."

"That's it?"

"That's it."

"Can I have that in writing?"

Give me your email and you'll have it within ten minutes."

"Fine. You'll have my answer shortly."

CHAPTER THIRTY ONE

NORA SPEAKS

The cause of death was suicide. A note was found by the body along with a printed copy of Mike's email offer of clemency. Evidently Fordney wanted it read in conjunction with his note, an apology which he couldn't bring himself to write.

The note said: "I am leaving. Without John my life is barren. He died in my arms. As we were together in life, I now wish to be with him in death. I had hoped to make of his death one final statement on the fatal error I believe our government is making with Russia. Russia will never be our friend. I have failed in that, not because the message is erroneous, but because my efforts were miscast. John deserved better. I leave with only that regret."

Prime Minister James D Stevens rose on the floor of the House of Representatives.

"Mr. Speaker, It is my pleasure to announce that in two weeks we will be receiving a visit from the Foreign Minister of the Russian Federal Republic, Mr. Maximus Smyrnov, to put the final touches on a treaty of Friendship and Amity between the United States and the Federated Russian Republic."

He held up his hand to forestall the objection from Congressman Spurlock, rising that moment, an accusation at the ready.

"To answer the accusation I see frothing at the lips of the honorable member from Kentucky, let me assure him we are not welcoming in our midst one who presumes to murder American citizens on our own soil. Mr. Spurlock, I can see, is about to refer once more to the case of John Stapelton whose body was found some weeks ago in front of the Treasury with Novichok present on his lips. Mr. Spurlock continues to insist this proves Russia is responsible for Mr. Stapelton' death.

"As in so much else, Mr. Spurlock is wrong. I can now inform this house that the Metropolitan Police and this government are in possession of facts to show how deeply in error he has been.

"As the coroner's report has already established, Mr. Stapelton died of a heart attack, not Novichok. Novichok was smeared on his lips after his death.

"The only questions were, who smeared the Novichok on him, and why?

"We now have the answers. The Novichok was put on Mr. Stapelton' body by one Paul Fordney, a close personal friend of Stapleton's, to mislead the public into thinking it the work of Russia. Mr. Fordney, a retired CIA officer with experience in Russian affairs, disagreed profoundly with our efforts to improve relations with Russia and sought to undermine those efforts in any way he could.

"The full facts of the case will be appearing shortly in a Washington Post story.

"We are prepared to brief any member of this house, including the right honorable member from Kentucky, on the facts and circumstances that brought the Metropolitan Police and the government to these conclusions."

"Got time for lunch?" Mike asked.

"When?"

"Today."

"Yeah, sure," Ralph said. "Where?"

"The Viking, in Georgetown. Know it?"

"Yeah, I know it. But it's way out of my league. Got a second choice?"

"No. My treat."

"You're shittin me, right?"

"No, no. Straight skinny."

"That place is expense account country. You get a special appropriation from Congress for this?"

Ralph laughed. To a policeman's salary, the Viking, which was more Georgetown than Georgetown, was as distant as the Himalayas.

"No, the PM expressly told me to take you there for lunch, his way of thanking you for your help. He also enjoyed your visit last week. Said he found your views and the way you expressed them refreshing. So we're serious. Now are you going to be a hardass about this or what?"

Ralph laughed again. "OK, I'm persuaded. What time?"

"Twelve thirty?"

"OK. See you then. But, hey, one thing. Do I need a coat and tie?"

"Why, you don't own a tie?"

"Yeah, smart ass, I got one somewhere."

"It's OK. No tie. It's casual at lunch time."

"See you twelve thirty."

Mike got there early. He was shown the best table in the house. The Prime Minister's secretary called ahead to make sure a table was available. The maître'd assured her the Viking's best table was there for the pleasure of the PM's party.

Ralph arrived shortly after Mike and slid into his seat.

"Now this is class," he said, suggesting all along he had been urging Mike to upgrade.

"Glad you approve. Drinks first?"

"I'm still on duty."

"You can't have a drink?"

"Didn't say that. Just said I'm on duty."

"Okay, but you're the Prime Minister's guest. I think the department can make an exception."

"What are you having?"

"A vodka Martini."

"Sounds good," Ralph said. "Make it two."

They sipped their drinks and ordered. Since the PM's office was paying, they both ordered sirloin. Mike got a baked potato with sour cream (he knew he'd have to report to Louise what they had for lunch at the Viking) and Ralph got fries.

"I'm still curious about one thing. How did Fordney manage to persuade Tabidze to give him the Novichok? Thought they kept that stuff under strict control."

"They do, but Tabidze was the controller. When the army CID finally leaned on Tabidze he came clean."

"So what was the story?"

""he PM' It' crime, yu do the timeIt's involved and some of it is classified. But the Pentagon is making a full report to the PM's office, so I'm not telling you anything you won't know anyway.

"Tabidze was a CIA asset for a number of years, passing on sensitive information about Russia's biological warfare program. Fordney was his control when he was station chief in Moscow. It was Fordney who got Tabidze out, the extraction, as they call it. Tabidze wasn't under direct suspicion so he could leave the country the way any Russian citizen could. Officially, he took a vacation and decided not to come back."

"And they bought that?"

"Maybe not, but absent any hard proof to the contrary, all they had were unconfirmed suspicions. You know better than I, these aren't the old days anymore. Then Tabidze would be seen as a defector with all that involved. Now he was just a guy who preferred the greener grass on the other side. "

"Okay, but how did Fordney manage to talk Tabidze into giving him the Novichok?"

"That's where all the ambiguities come in. Tabidze still has family in Russia. Fordney told him if it got out that Tabidze had been a CIA asset, there could be consequences for his family. That was enough to sway Tabidze. He gave Fordney a small vial of Novichok, but warned him if anyone turned up dead by Novichok he'd go to the authorities. He did not want any deaths on his conscience. Fordney assured him the Novichok was to be used to make a political statement, not to kill anyone. Tabidze felt he was in no position to resist, so he went along. After all, Fordney was his old control. "

They topped the meal off with a cognac in true celebration.

Mike said, "Couldn't have done this without your help. That speeding ticket was the key. He raised his glass. "A sincere thanks from us. You made an important contribution to changing US Russian relations for the better. America owes you."

"Like I said, it's just a question of turning over the rocks."

Mike got the other part of Tabidze's story, things Ralph wouldn't have known, from the Pentagon.

Tabidze would not be charged with a crime though he had violated several criminal statutes in giving the Novichok to an unauthorized person. A threat to his family, credible in his mind, was taken as a mitigating circumstance. But he could no longer be kept in his sensitive position at Fort Detrick. His name was not mentioned publically, but Russian intelligence was good at winkling out such details. Things might be changing in Russia, but betrayal might still be taken seriously by certain quarters of the Russian intelligence community. Tabidze was given a new identity and moved to an undisclosed part of the country to begin a new life.

Mike and Louise spent three days at Camp David enjoying the crisp fall air and foliage while Prime Minister Stevens and Foreign Minister strolled the brightly colored forest paths of the Camp. Smyrnov proudly showed pictures of his grandchildren and teased Stevens that he needed to nudge his daughter and that assistant of his to rectify matters.

Elam and Nora were there as well, part of Smyrnov's official party, invited by the PM to enjoy the week end. Elam looked around and said to Mike, "nice dacha."

Smyrnov's visit was concluded by a cultural evening at the Russian embassy. The first part was a concert by a visiting Russian pianist performing Russian and American music, including pieces by Tchaikovsky, Shostakovich, Copeland and Gershwin.

The second part consisted or a reading of Russian poetry by Nora. She read from a poem by Osip Mandelshtam which contained the passage:

We shall meet again in Petersburg
As though we had interred the sun in it
And shall pronounce for the first time
That blessed, senseless word . . .
She looked up, found Louise's eyes, and said, "Peace."

May 1, 2019 Lexington, Kentucky